DYSPHAGIA COOKBOOK

Delicious, Easy-to-Swallow, and Soft-Food Recipes
for People with Swallowing and Chewing difficulty with
a 30-Day Meal Plan Included

By

EMILY JOHNSON

© Copyright 2023 by Emily Johnson – All rights reserved

This document is geared towards providing exact and reliable information regarding the topic and issue covered. The publication is sold with the idea that the publisher is not required to render accounting, officially permitted, or otherwise, qualified services. If advice is necessary, legal or professional, a practiced individual in the profession should be ordered.

From a Declaration of Principles which was accepted and approved equally by a Committee of the American Bar Association and a Committee of Publishers and Associations.

In no way is it legal to reproduce, duplicate, or transmit any part of this document in either electronic means or in printed format. Recording of this publication is strictly prohibited and any storage of this document is not allowed unless with written permission from the publisher. All rights reserved.

The information provided herein is stated to be truthful and consistent, in that any liability, in terms of inattention or otherwise, by any usage or abuse of any policies, processes, or directions contained within is the solitary and utter responsibility of the recipient reader. Under no circumstances will any legal responsibility or blame be held against the publisher for any reparation, damages, or monetary loss due to the information herein, either directly or indirectly.

Respective authors own all copyrights not held by the publisher.

The information herein is offered for informational purposes solely and is universal as so. The presentation of the information is without a contract or any type of guarantee assurance.

The trademarks that are used are without any consent, and the publication of the trademark is without permission or backing by the trademark owner. All trademarks and brands within this book are for clarifying purposes only and are owned by the owners themselves, not affiliated with this document.

TABLE OF CONTENTS

Introduction 1

Chapter 1: Introduction to Dysphagia 3
    1.1 Defining Dysphagia 3
    1.2 Why a Dysphagia Diet is Needed 4
    1.3 Foods to Choose and Avoid 6
    1.4 Causes of Dysphagia 8
    1.5 Dysphagia's Psychological Aspects 10
    1.6 Psychiatric Causes of Dysphagia 11
    1.7 Degree of Dysphagia 13
    1.8 Home Treatment for Dysphagia Swallowing Activities 15
    1.9 Seven Recommendations for Properly Handling Dysphagia at Home 17
    1.10 Support as a Caregiver 19
    1.11 Ten Strategies for Easier Mealtimes with Dysphagia 21

Chapter 2: Breakfast Recipes 22
    1. Pureed Sausage Gravy and Biscuits 23
    2. Pureed Berry Muffins 23
    3. Thickened Brown Sugar Milk Tea 24
    4. Apple, Squash, and Turkey Sausage Hash (Moist and Minced) 25
    5. Basted Eggs 26
    6. Coconut Mango Puree 27
    7. 7. Bread Stuffing 27
    8. Cranberry Almond Bread 28
    9. Cranberry Pear Tart 29
    10. Pureed Broccoli, Cheese, and Egg Dish 30
    11. Chocolate Avocado Pudding 31
    12. Apple Crumble 32
    13. Baked Custard 32
    14. Maple Sweet Carrot Puree 33

15. Pumpkin Brownie Puree 34
16. Peach Apricot Puree 34
17. Fig Berry Puree 35
18. Peaches and Cream 36
19. Frozen Yogurt Parfait 36
20. Scrambled Egg and Bean Puree 37
21. Pureed Egg Salad 38
22. Scrambled Eggs 38

Chapter 3: Lunch Recipes 39

1. Fresh Pea Soup 40
2. Lima Bean Purée 40
3. Pumpkin Cauliflower Curry 41
4. Chili 42
5. Chicken a la King 43
6. Turkey Tetrazzini 43
7. Pureed Pasta with Beef Marinara 44
8. Vegetable Fried Rice 45
9. Hamburger and Bun 45
10. Pureed Cornbread 46
11. Beef Stroganoff 47
12. Minced Turkey Tetrazzini 48
13. Corned Beef and Cabbage 48
14. White Sauce Pasta Recipe 49
15. Pureed Lemon Cream Cheese Pie 50
16. Meat Loaf Puree 51
17. Chicken Tikka Masala with Sticky Rice 52
18. Roasted Cauliflower Macaroni and Cheese 53
19. Black Bean Soup 54
20. Italian Chicken Puree 55
21. Black Bean and Red Pepper Puree 55
22. Pureed Salmon 56
23. Sausage and Onions 57

Chapter 4: Dinner Recipes 58

1. Easy-Peasy Chicken 59
2. Lobster Bisque 59
3. Beef and Sweet Potato Puree with Thyme 60
4. Minced Meat Shepherd's Pie 60
5. Soft Potatoes 61
6. Pureed Pasta with Chicken Alfredo 62
7. Sweet and Sour Chicken 63
8. Country BBQ Sundae 63
9. BBQ Pork 64
10. Spiced Carrot and Lentil Soup 65
11. Cullen Skink 66
12. Pureed Green Bean Casserole 67
13. Pureed Lasagna 67
14. Hash of Turkey Sausage 68
15. Pureed Cheesy Vegetable Dish 69
16. Creamy Fortified Butternut Squash Soup 70
17. Turkey and Dumpling Soup 71
18. Macaroni and Cheese 71
19. Cold-Day Chicken Noodle Soup 72
20. Potatoes with Cheddar 73
21. Grilled Cheese and Pickle Sandwich 74
22. Braised Carrots 75
23. Lyonnaise Potatoes 75
24. Turkey Burgers with Roasted Sweet Potatoes 76
25. Chicken Croquettes with Mashed Potatoes 77
26. Pumpkin Crisp 78
27. Tangy Chicken Salad 79
28. Basic Fish Puree 80
29. Pureed Beef Stew 80
30. Tuna and Beans Puree 81
31. Chicken and Sweet Potato Puree 82

Chapter 5: Snacks and Desert Recipes 83

1. Savory Beet Puree 84
2. Sweet Apple Bread Puree 85
3. Decadent Dessert 85
4. Watermelon Sorbet 86
5. Minted Melon Smoothie 86
6. Vanilla Cake 87
7. Chocolate Cake 88
8. Thickened Mocha Latte 88
9. Thickened Pumpkin Spice Latte 89
10. Watermelon Lime Sorbet 90
11. Luck of the Irish Milkshake 91
12. Lava Cakes 91
13. Snickerdoodle Cookies 92
14. Pureed Peanut Butter Blossom Cookies 93
15. Pureed Vanilla Cream Cheese Pumpkin Squares 94
16. Bolognese Sauce 95
17. Creamy Garlic Cauliflower Puree 95
18. Pureed Macaroni and Cheese 96
19. Pureed Cauliflower 96
20. Maple Sweet Potato 97
21. Cream of Broccoli Soup 97
22. Banana Protein Shake 98
23. Strawberry Protein Shake 99

Chapter 6: 30-Day Meal Plan 100

Conclusion 106

Conversion Table 108

INTRODUCTION

An individual swallows food about six hundred times per day. Four phases, 25 distinct muscles, and five nerves are involved in every swallow. Many people eat and drink for free, but some people battle regularly with these fundamental skills. Dysphagia, or problems with swallowing, can be brought on by some conditions, including physiological, neural, anatomical, or drug-related ones. As a result, each beloved one has unique requirements and worries, particularly in social situations. A loved one might get reluctant to appear in public or at a family meeting due to humiliation from losing control or curious observers. As a caretaker, it's crucial to maintain a loved one's belief in self and freedom while also supporting them as digestive issues develop.

Dysphagia refers to a problem ingesting or digesting food or liquids. Food has to first be fully chewed. By contracting the facial muscles and pushing the tongue toward the top of the mouth, it is then shifted to the rear of the mouth. The process then goes into automated mode; it is a reaction that individuals do not consciously regulate. The soft palate stops the nasal passage to stop food from reversing into it, the airways of the lungs are closed, and the esophagus softens to let food and fluids enter. Then, in a wave-like motion, the muscle esophagus closes, moving the food to the stomach. Dysphagia can be caused by an obstruction or a failure in any place in this area of our bodies or in the nerve system that regulates eating. Making the correct diagnosis is the first stage in the healing process. Often, therapy must be approached collaboratively. The finest program is created in collaboration with a variety of healthcare professionals, including certified dietitians, speech pathologists, psychologists, and physical therapists.

Being capable of securely ingesting food and liquids comes in the first place when considering eating objectives for individuals with dysphagia. The second thing is making sure they receive proper nourishment, which is crucial for their life, healing, and/or general well-being. However, while enjoyment of meals with loved ones or companions is crucial for a person's general safety, quality of life and dietary worth are also key considerations. Mealtimes ought to be happy, carefree, and pleasant events. Therefore, it must be a top goal to make meals and beverages enjoyable so they taste great and appear appetizing.

Chapter 1

Introduction to Dysphagia

In this chapter, you will learn about dysphagia, its symptoms, and its causes. Further, the psychological aspect of dysphagia is discussed in detail. Food to eat and avoid are listed properly. Some tips and tricks for caregivers and other suggestions to improve the life of the person having dysphagia are also described in detail.

1.1 Defining Dysphagia

Dysphagia is a term in medicine that is used to describe the difficulty in swallowing and the pain that we experience during swallowing. Mostly, in this condition, people have difficulty swallowing particular liquids or foods, but some cannot even swallow their saliva. When this happens, eating food becomes challenging for most of us. Mostly, it becomes difficult for us to take in enough calories and fluids for the nourishment of our body, and this can cause other serious problems. Dysphagia is primarily found in our elderly as their muscles weaken as time passes, and they're more expected to become prone to illnesses that result in dysphagia. Problems with dysphagia that are mostly seen in people are dehydration, malnutrition, as well as respiratory infections. Dysphagia should be taken seriously because those who can't swallow properly cannot eat enough food to stay fit or keep a model weight. But don't worry; by having a dysphagia diet and eating easy-to-swallow food, we can become healthy and fit.

Symptoms

Below I will tell you about some symptoms and signs that we normally see in dysphagia patients:

- » Incapability to swallow
- » Painful swallowing

- Hoarseness
- Drooling
- Gagging or coughing when swallowing
- Regurgitation
- Stomach acid or food backing up in your throat
- Frequent heartburn
- A feeling of food stuck in your chest or throat or behind your breastbone
- Weight loss

1.2 Why a Dysphagia Diet is Needed

I know how difficult it becomes for us to maintain our weight and keep our body healthy with dysphagia, but with the right diet and food consistency, it becomes easy to overcome these problems. You are more likely to aspirate if you have dysphagia. When liquid or food accidentally gets into the lungs, it's called aspiration. It may result in pneumonia or other issues. Your capacity to swallow might be affected by the foods that you consume. For instance, soft meals are simpler to engulf than hard ones. Aspiration may be avoided with a dysphagia diet. You might be in danger of aspiration due to dysphagia if you possess any of the following medical conditions:

- Severe dental issues
- Stroke
- Mouth sores
- Radiation treatment or throat cancer surgery
- Sjogren's syndrome, which causes less saliva to produce
- Blockage in the esophagus, like growth from cancer
- Neurological problems such as Parkinson's disease
- Muscular dystrophies

You may only need to adhere to a dysphagia meal for a brief period of time. Or you could spend some time on it. It varies according to the kind and severity of your dysphagia.

Dysphagia Diet Levels

A diet strategy for those who have dysphagia has been developed by the Academy of Nutrition and Dietetics. The National Dysphagia Diet is the name of the program. There are four food levels in the dysphagia diet. Levels include:

- **Level 1.** These are smooth or pureed meals, such as pudding. No need to chew them. Yogurt, potatoes mashed with gravy to provide moisture, silky soups, and pureed meats and vegetables are examples of dishes that fall under this category.

- » **Level 2.** These meals are wet and require some chewing. These consist of mashed, cooked, or soft vegetables or fruits, soft or ground meats drenched in gravy, peanut butter, cottage cheese, and soft eggs that have been scrambled. Nuts, crackers, and all other dry foods should be avoided.
- » **Level 3.** It consists of chewing-intensive soft-solid meals. This includes cut-or-mashable meat, fruit, and veggies. Avoid meals that are very dry, sticky, or crunchy. This applies to snacks like almonds, chips, crackers, and other things.
- » **Level 4.** Foods at every level are included in level 4.

Additionally, you will need to exercise caution while consuming beverages.

Preparing Food and liquids

Preparing food and drinks for yourself or as a caregiver for the dysphagia patients is a crucial work to do when dealing with dysphagia. You might have to cut down on or alter your intake of certain foods. You may have to purée your meals, for instance. Before blending your food, be sure that you taste and season it. If the food tastes good and smells good, it will be simpler to stick to a healthy diet.

Liquids could also have to be thickened. Your liquids may be controlled by thickening thin liquids. Mixing it with a flavorless powder, gum, gel, or some other kind of fluid is accomplished. They are thickening agents. Also available are pre-thickened drinks.

While Eating

It could be beneficial to sit up with a straight back when eating or drinking. To get the ideal posture, you may require support cushions. Having minimal distractions when drinking or eating might be beneficial. Your swallowing may also benefit from alternating between solid meals and liquids. After eating, remain upright until at least 30 minutes. Aspiration risk may be lowered as a result of this.

Keep an eye out for aspiration signs like:

- » Wheezing or coughing during eating or shortly after
- » Excessive salivation
- » Breathing difficulty or exhaustion during eating
- » A moist voice while, after, or in the hours after eating
- » Fever

After Eating

It's crucial to practice good dental hygiene after eating. When doing your oral hygiene regimen, be careful not to ingest any water.

1.3 Foods to Choose and Avoid

Following is the list of foods that I mostly choose in my diet and those at I have been avoiding. You should choose your food items carefully when eating when you are suffering from dysphagia.

Vegetables and fruits

Foods that are better for you:

- Finely minced or shredded salads (leafy greens, coleslaw, lettuce) with additional dressing if desirable
- Soft cooked diced vegetables (squash, carrots), cooked mashable vegetables (spinach, peas), or cooked minced vegetables (green or yellow beans, broccoli)
- Mashed potatoes or properly cooked potato dishes like scalloped potatoes
- Fruit smoothies
- Mashable soft and ripe fruit: fresh, canned, or frozen (canned pineapple, mandarin oranges, sliced peaches, or ripe pears, bananas), fresh fruit having skins and membranes removed (seedless watermelon, soft cantaloupe) fruit cocktail having no grapes or pineapple pieces
- Canned cream corn
- Stewed, pureed pitted prunes

Foods that you should avoid:

- Tossed salad made with components that are not allowed
- Hard and raw vegetables which are not mashable (carrot sticks, broccoli, celery, cauliflower), even diced
- Salad or cabbage which is not shredded (spinach, Caesar, tossed)
- Pineapple, canned or fresh, chunks, sliced, or tidbits
- Kernel corn, whole, even not in soup
- Crispy and dry French fries, potato skins, or hash browns
- Canned or fresh fruits or vegetables with tough skins or membranes (whole tomatoes, citrus fruits, whole apples, grapes)
- Dry fruit (cranberries, coconut, raisins)
- Fruits having hard seeds (raspberries, blackberries)

Grain Foods

Foods that are better for you:

- Cold cereals which get soft in milk (corn flakes, bran flakes, rice crisps)
- Cooked cereals (oat bran, cream of rice, oatmeal)
- Pancakes, French toast, or waffles with syrup or applesauce to moisten
- Ground wheat bran or flax seed mixed into cereals

- » Soft bread products (buns, buttered toast, biscuits, muffins) served using soft margarine, butter or allowed spreads
- » Soft, moist couscous, barley, quinoa, or rice in soups, sauces, or casseroles, pasta in sauce
- » Soft crackers, like soda crackers
- » Bread pudding or moist and soft bread stuffing (without coconut, dried fruit, chocolate chips, seeds, nuts, or hard particles)
- » Soft textured cereal bars, like bars

Foods that you should avoid:

- » Crusty, chewy, or dry bread (crusty buns, bagels, pitas, English muffins, tortillas)
- » Dry pizza crust, for example, thin crust pizza
- » grain or cereals products (with coconut, chocolate chips, nuts, dried fruit, or seeds)
- » Chewy or hard cereal bars, granola or crackers
- » Loose and dry rice (fried, brown, wild, steamed)

Protein Foods

Foods that are better for you:

- » Smooth milkshakes, buttermilk, or soy beverages that are fortified
- » Flavored or plain milk
- » Cottage cheese
- » Fruit yogurt or smooth yogurt having soft small fruit pieces
- » All cheeses (soft or hard), sliced, diced, or grated
- » Soft-cooked lentils, beans, soft dishes, or peas made with permissible ingredients (soft bean salad)
- » Soy protein/soft tofu
- » Nut butter which is smooth, mixed into permitted foods (smoothie of peanut butter)
- » Soft, moist, and tender poultry or meat, diced
- » All egg substitutes or cooked eggs, including quiche and omelets, used with foods that are allowed
- » Canned fish having bones taken out (canned salmon having mashed bones)
- » Thinly soft shaved deli meats (turkey, roast beef, ham)
- » Boneless tender flaked fish
- » Broth or cream soups with ingredients that are allowed
- » Sandwiches having finely-minced salad-type fillings (chicken, egg, minced lettuce, tuna salad, or cheese) that have no whole raw vegetables or lettuce
- » Soft and mashable pierogies with condiments that are allowed
- » Mashable tender meats, with ingredients that are allowed (casseroles, shepherd's pie, lasagna stir-fry with ingredients that are allowed
- » Spaghetti sauces with ingredients that are allowed

Foods that you should avoid:

- » Melting string cheese with a crunchy topping (for instance, on casserole)
- » Yogurt (with huge fruit pieces, nuts, dried fruit, seeds, or granola)
- » Nut butter, which may be put on meals and are either crunchy or creamy
- » Hard-fried eggs
- » Chopped or whole nuts or seeds
- » Wieners or hamburgers on buns
- » Bacon, beef jerky, or bacon bits
- » Chili, casseroles, or stews with ingredients that are prohibited
- » Dry or crispy meat, fish, or poultry
- » Processed sausages, luncheon meats, or wieners having hard casings, like Kolbassa, salami, or garlic sausage

Desserts and Snacks

Foods that are better for you:

- » Frozen yogurt, sherbet, Popsicles, or frozen soy desserts
- » Soft, moist, or breakable biscuits
- » Smooth custards, mousse, milk pudding, tapioca pudding, or rice pudding (digestive biscuits)
- » Soft-baked treats prepared with permitted ingredients, such as moist cakes and pumpkin pies
- » Desserts made with jam

Foods that you should avoid:

- » Custards, puddings, or baked goods containing dried fruit, seeds, nuts, or chocolate chips
- » hard or crispy or snacks and desserts
- » pretzels, nachos, popcorn, or chips
- » Toffee, licorice, hard candies, or gum

1.4 Causes of Dysphagia

We know that dysphagia is caused by any abnormality in our throat or esophagus. Dysphagia may be brought on by any disorder that impairs or harms the swallowing muscles and nerves or that causes the throat or esophagus to narrow.

Generally speaking, dysphagia fits into any of these groups.

1) Esophageal Dysphagia

Esophageal dysphagia is the term used to describe the feeling that food is stuck or is becoming lodged in the chest or base of the throat after you have begun to swallow.

- **Achalasia.** Esophageal dysphagia may have a variety of reasons. Food may come again into the throat when your sphincter fails to relax sufficiently to allow food to reach the stomach. It's also possible that the esophageal wall's muscles are weak, an issue that seems to become worse with time.
- **Diffuse spasm.** This syndrome causes your esophagus to constrict at high pressure and with poor coordination, often after eating. The lower esophageal walls' involuntary muscles are affected by diffuse spasms.
- **Esophagus stricture.** Large chunks of food might become stuck in your constricted esophagus. The narrowing may be brought on by tumors or scar tissue, both of which are often brought on by GERD (gastroesophageal reflux disease).
- **Esophageal tumors.** Due to constriction of the esophagus brought on by esophageal tumors, swallowing difficulties in people like us often grow progressively worse.
- **Foreign bodies.** The esophagus or throat may sometimes get partly blocked by food or something else. Meal fragments becoming stuck in one's-esophagus or throat may be more likely to happen to older folks with dentures and those who have trouble chewing their meals.
- **Esophageal ring.** Off and on having trouble swallowing solid meals might be a result of a thin region of constriction in your lower esophagus.
- **GERD.** Lower esophageal spasm, scarring, and constriction may result from harm to tissues of the esophagus brought on by stomach acid flowing back into the esophagus.
- **Esophagitis with eosinophilia.** This illness is brought on by an overabundance of eosinophils in the esophagus, which may be connected to an allergy to certain foods.
- **Scleroderma.** The lower esophageal sphincter may become less effective due to the growth of scar-like material that causes tissues to stiffen and harden. As a consequence, acid builds up and often causes heartburn in the esophagus.
- **Radiation treatment.** The esophagus may become inflamed and scarred as a result of this cancer therapy.

2) oropharyngeal dysphagia

When you begin to swallow, it may be challenging to transport food from the mouth into the esophagus and throat due to weak muscles in the throat caused by certain disorders. When trying to swallow, you could feel as if food or liquids are entering your trachea or traveling up your nose, causing you to gag, choke, or cough. This may result in pneumonia.

It can be caused by:

> » Oropharyngeal dysphagia may be brought on by neurological conditions. Dysphagia may be brought on by many conditions, including Parkinson's disease, muscular dystrophy, and multiple sclerosis.
> » Neurological injury. The capacity to swallow may be impacted by sudden neurological impairment, such as that caused by a stroke, brain injury, or spinal cord injury.
> » Zenker's diverticulum, or pharyngoesophageal diverticulum. A tiny pouch within the throat, often immediately above the esophagus, that develops and gathers food particles causes difficulties swallowing, gurgling noises, poor breath, and frequent throat clearing or coughing.
> » Cancer. The inability to swallow may be brought on by some tumors and cancer therapies like radiotherapy.

1.5 Dysphagia's Psychological Aspects

Appreciating Dysphagia's Detrimental Psychological Consequences

According to research, dysphagia may ruin social chances and the enjoyment of meals, have an impact on patients' connections to their families and caregivers, and be detrimental to their physical and mental health. This is mostly because the patient needs help eating or is embarrassed about having eating issues. Dysphagia patients may experience social exclusion, a sense of being left out, anxiety, and discomfort, particularly around mealtimes. This may thus have a harmful impact on a patient's self-esteem, dignity, and capacity to maintain fulfilling personal connections and an active life.

Patients with dysphagia who exhibit signs of sadness, seclusion, and rejection of the disease may sometimes suffer psychological, interpersonal, and bodily harm. In one research, a sample of individuals was used. Almost 1/2 of them were under 60 years old, remained actively employed, and had a lively social life. These individuals were shown to be more fragile, lacking confidence in themselves, restricting their social interactions, and subsequently having the propensity to isolate themselves after receiving a dysphagia diagnosis. While the majority of research participants no more saw mealtimes as an enjoyable pleasurable part of their daily lives because of their recent swallowing issues, a lot of patients used to think of times of eating as a chance to socialize and encounter others.

Patients with dysphagia often hide or reject their disease while they are in this mental state. According to one research, just 36% of those surveyed recognized obtaining a verified dysphagia diagnosis while only 32% said they got professional therapy for their problem. Patients were not likely to approach healthcare providers or family members on their own to discuss their swallowing issues unless encouraged by a family member.

Recognizing and Meeting the Psychological Requirements of Patients with Dysphagia

Although those with dysphagia might be reluctant to admit to having the problem, it is crucial to look for its warning signs to ensure the right treatments may be provided. Health practitioners may prevent the individual's psychological, social, and bodily harm by informing the patient, evaluating the patient in relation to a variety of other diseases and issues, and offering the client the right dysphagia treatment choices.

According to studies, people with dysphagia often retreat mentally as a result of feeling powerless against their sickness. Dysphagia sufferers may reduce stress, gain confidence in the healing process, and develop a more optimistic attitude about their health by having a network of healthcare specialists who can give information on efficient treatment alternatives.

After being educated by physicians and healthcare professionals about typical psychological problems associated with dysphagia, patients' lives were qualitatively improved. Through rehabilitation treatment, they were also able to enhance their swallowing.

A Well-Informed Patient Is More Mentally Satisfied

According to widely accepted studies, healthcare providers should arm those who have a variety of knowledge and tools for recognizing and managing dysphagia so that they may live more easily and stress-free.

For them to collaborate and offer the patient quick and efficient support aimed at enhancing their quality of life, medical professionals must be conscious of and more knowledgeable about this issue through information exchange, especially with relatives close to the patient.

1.6 Psychiatric Causes of Dysphagia

People may have dysphagia for a variety of causes. However, among those who have functional dysphagia, mental health issues are a relatively common cause. I'll tell you what mental disorders cause dysphagia. We should be careful with these disorders:

- » Posttraumatic stress disorder (PTSD)
- » Obsessive-compulsive disorder (OCD)

- » Depression
- » Social phobias
- » Panic disorder
- » Generalized anxiety disorder (GAD)

These people may have dysphagia as a consequence of SSD (somatic-symptom disorder), a condition marked by excessive attention to physical symptoms that interferes with everyday tasks.

If a person exhibits a minimum of the following traits, they may be identified as having SSD:

- » Severe anxiety due to health
- » Consistent, inflated worries about the extent of health condition
- » An excessive focus on health issues

Dysphagia may occasionally—though this is uncommon—be a fear. These fears consist of:

- » **Phagophobia:** Anxiety of swallowing brought on by a psychological cause instead of a physical one.
- » **Pseudo dysphagia:** Anxiety of choking.

Since they have problems sitting still while eating, some people with mental disorders may have periods of dysphagia. This increases the likelihood that food can become lodged. Or, they eat too rapidly because they are very active.

Experts have discovered a considerable correlation in recent years between anxiety and the seriousness of dysphagia symptoms. "Esophageal hypervigilance," a strong, excessive concentration on swallowing, may be brought on by anxiety. Individuals who received treatment for an esophageal ailment are more likely to experience it.

Treatment for a Mental Health Issue

As I have already mentioned above that the reason for dysphagia affects the course of treatment. Treatment options, if it has a mental etiology, include:

- » Medicine adjustment: For patients with mental problems in whom dysphagia could be a side effect, healthcare professionals may reduce the dosage or test a different medicine.
- » Cognitive behavioral treatment (CBT), hypnotherapy, or relaxation therapy are examples of psychotherapy or behavioral treatment.
- » Chewing and swallowing treatment is sometimes used in conjunction with psychotherapy.

If You Struggle with Anxiety, How Are You Able to Handle Swallowing Issues?

When you're feeling anxious, psychotherapy may be useful, but there are additional self-help techniques that may be beneficial. When you are battling with swallowing fear, mindfulness, deep breathing, meditation, and gradual relaxation of muscles might help reduce anxiety. Discuss the treatment options with a medical practitioner.

1.7 Degree of Dysphagia

Dysphagia can have 4 degrees that are based on where the swallowing impairment occurs: oropharyngeal, esophagogastric, esophageal, and paraesophageal.

1. Oropharyngeal Dysphagia

When it is difficult to transfer bolus from the oral cavity to the cervical esophagus, this condition is known as oropharyngeal dysphagia. A synchronized voluntary transport of food from the mouth into the pharynx is necessary for normal oropharyngeal swallowing, which is followed by a quick transfer of bolus into the upper esophagus. The symptoms are related to problems starting or delivering a liquid or solid meal bolus. This might involve pulmonary aspiration signs in addition to the perception (and occurrence) of a meal sticking in the mouth or neck area. This kind of dysphagia is caused by a variety of neuromuscular problems, which make up 75–85% of the causes. Such aberrations may also be brought on by oropharyngeal anatomical malformations. Some malformations result from faults in the oral cavity, jaw, and pharynx development. The upper esophageal sphincter's malfunction is the most frequent cause. The top esophageal sphincter's inability to relax or failure of relaxation to coincide with pharyngeal contraction can lead to this failure.

2. Esophageal Dysphagia

Esophageal dysphagia, which affects the area between the upper and lower esophageal sphincters, is characterized by difficulties swallowing solid or liquid substances. It comes from either physical obstruction to passage or aberrant motility of this section of the esophagus (obstruction). Normal esophageal peristalsis needs smoothly synchronized muscular activation in a single region with muscle relaxation in surrounding segments, albeit the processes behind this process are not entirely understood. The cause of esophageal disturbance will determine the symptoms, even if they are related to disordered meal transport. Dysphagia will accompany motility difficulties for both liquids and solids. There is no esophageal lumen shortening and no esophageal constriction.

Abnormalities in the frequency of contractions, speed, force, coordinated timing, or a combination of these factors are indicative of motility disorders. As a consequence, symptoms such as spasms or chest discomfort may also be present along with dysphagia. The trouble swallowing food is usually higher and manifests sooner than the problem swallowing liquids when a physical blockage is the source of dysphagia. When the esophageal lumen is reduced by approximately 12 mm, severe dysphagia for solids often develops. Dysphagia for fluids may develop simultaneously with dysphagia for solids, or it can occur until the esophageal lumen has shrunk by 50% or more.

3. Esophagogastric Dysphagia

Esophagogastric dysphagia happens when a physical or motor barrier prevents food from passing through the inferior esophageal sphincter and into the gastric fundus. Lower esophageal sphincter anomalies, benign or cancerous distal esophageal strictures, and gastric cardia mass lesions are some of the reasons. Due to insufficient relaxation of the sphincter muscle adjacent to the distal esophagus and stomach, dysphagia results from inferior esophageal sphincter high blood pressure, which is defined by achalasia. At the lower part of the sternum, it gives the impression that food is clinging. Odynophagia and chest discomfort brought on by strong non-propulsive esophageal contractions are two additional signs of motility problems. The regular flow of food into the stomach is impaired by mass lesions of the gastric cardia.

4. Paraoesophageal Dysphagia

When the esophagus wall and lumen are physically impinged upon or when penetration of the esophageal wall results in blockage, paraesophageal dysphagia develops. If severe, this might affect the esophagus's second motor function. Maintaining a clear and empty esophagus by eliminating acid from the stomach to come up is the second motor function of the esophagus.

1.8 Home Treatment for Dysphagia Swallowing Activities

Many home exercises are effective. Following are some exercises I mostly do at home and would like to recommend them to you as well.

1. Shaker Exercise

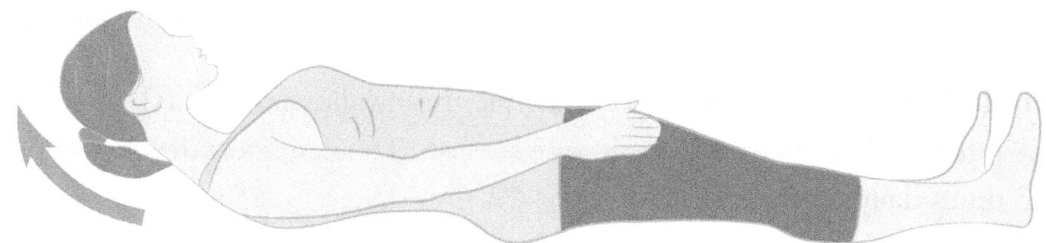

Goal: To build muscle and enhance your swallowing.

How to Do It: Start by lying flat on the back and lifting your head just a little bit off the floor. So that your gaze is fixed on the bottoms of your feet, elevate the top of your head sufficiently high. After a little period of holding this posture, lower your head again. Continue to move in this manner a couple more times. Perform this type of activity 3–6 times during the day to receive optimum benefits. You may lengthen the head raise and add more repetitions as you become stronger.

2. Hyoid Lift Maneuver

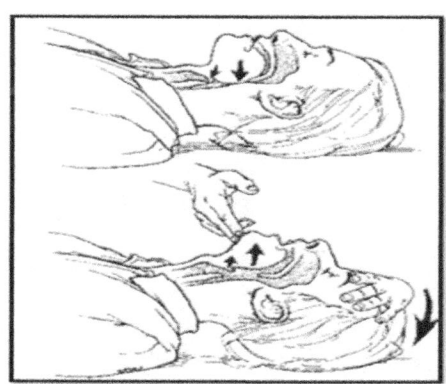

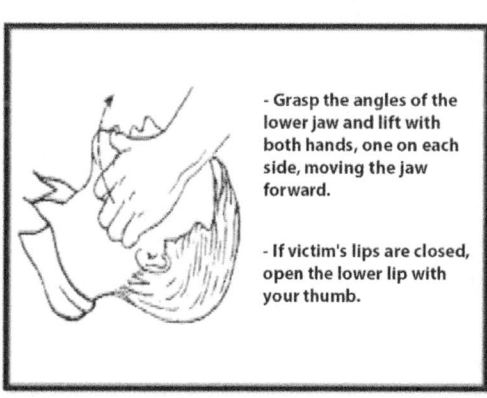

Goal: Strengthens and improves control of the swallowing muscles.

How to Do It: In the direction of you, spread out many little pieces of tissue paper on a towel. After that, put the straw in the mouth and suck on it, letting the straw's tip suck up paper. As you move the straw to a cup, continue sucking while doing so, then let go to let the paper fall into the cup. You should try to fill the cup with all the different pieces of paper. Start with 3 to five pieces of tissue paper and gradually increase to about ten.

3. Active Swallow

Goal: Intensify the interaction and synchronization of the various muscles utilized in swallowing.

How to Do It: Squeeze as hard as you can all the swallowing-related muscles during dry swallowing. Up to ten times may be done in one session. To adequately develop your muscles, do this activity 3 times daily.

4. Supraglottic Swallow

Goal: To make it easier to swallow meals.

How to Do It: As you insert a little mouthful of food in the mouth and consume it, inhale a long breath and continue to hold it. After that, cough to get rid of any saliva or food that may have gotten past your vocal cords. Exhale lastly. Don't eat while doing the workout the first few times. You may attempt this task with a little piece of something in your mouth if you've had enough experience with it.

5. The Super Supraglottic-Swallow Maneuver

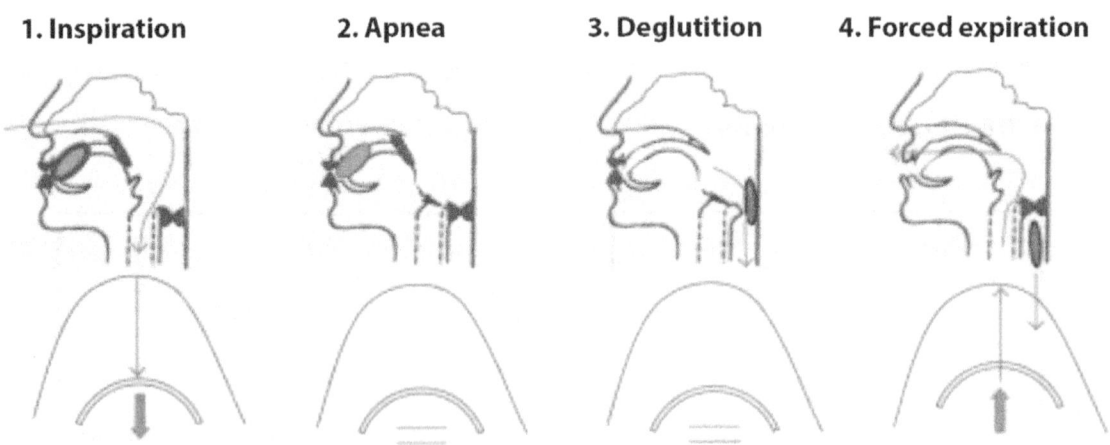

Goal: Improves food digestion and helps the muscles involved in swallowing.

The procedure for this task is essentially identical to the one for the prior one, just a bit more intensive. In this, you have to push through while inhaling deeply and swallowing forcefully.

1.9 Seven Recommendations for Properly Handling Dysphagia at Home

When you are dealing with a person who has dysphagia at home or as a caregiver, the following recommendation may be very helpful.

1. Thicken Pharmaceuticals Safely

Your elderly relative will now need to drink something thickened to take oral medicines that they previously took with water. Alternately, the tablets must be broken up and combined with a thicker meal, such as pudding or sauce. The majority of individuals find it difficult to bear the taste of crushed medications. It's usually a nice idea to use chocolate, applesauce, vanilla pudding, or anything else sweet to cover up the overpoweringly harsh taste of medicine.

2. Steer Clear of Straws

A speech therapist may inform you it's typically inappropriate for dysphagia sufferers to utilize straws based on the state of the person. Utilizing a straw might seem like a beneficial tool for somebody who suffers from problems drinking, but a straw is more probable to increase the amount of fluid in the mouth. It additionally makes it more challenging for muscles that are already weak to push the liquid through the right pipe, which might result in aspiration or choking.

3. Maintain Hydration

Anyone giving care to a dysphagia patient has to be well hydrated. Any water or beverage that has been diagnosed with dysphagia has to be thickened. Drinking liquids that have been thickened takes more time to consume than liquids that have not been thickened. Thus, maintaining optimal hydration demands patience as well as closer attention from you. Thickening agents, which are generally purchased at pharmacies or online, can be available as powders or gels that be blended with beverages.

4. Avoid Jell-O and Ice Cream

While ice cream and Jell-O may seem like traditional dessert options for older individuals, they are off-limits if related to the dysphagia diet. Jell-O and ice cream both can melt inside the mouth and convert into a thin fluid that, if ingested, might result in aspiration. Dysphagia causes the tongue and jaw to work harder and longer to transport food to the back of the throat when swallowing. As a result, foods like ice cream and Jell-O have more chances to melt in a potentially hazardous liquid.

5. Consume Enough Wholesome Food

Getting sufficient calories, minerals, and vitamins is a difficult struggle among numerous dysphagia sufferers. Drinks like Ensure and Boost might seem like a smart idea to substitute meals and add calories. However, due to the number of proteins and vitamins found inside the drink, it can be challenging to thicken them adequately. Additionally, they include a lot of sugar and artificial substances. There are additional strategies to include complete foods and nutritious components in a diet for people with dysphagia:

- » To enhance the number of calories and aid older persons in maintaining their weight, foods high in fat may be added to both savory and sweet meals. These foods include Greek yogurt, peanut butter, avocado, soft cheeses, and coconut cream.
- » Wintertime squash, beans (refried, cannellini, black, etc.), steamed veggies (cauliflower, kale, broccoli, spinach, etc.), and fruits (strawberries, banana, mango, etc.) are all readily pureed foods that add tons of essential nutrients to the adult's diet as well as can be added to thickened stews and purees.
- » Some dietitians may suggest adding powdered protein or beneficial drink blends (like Juven) to the diet to assist them to maintain weight, particularly those who are gaining muscle.
- » Milk may be blended in foods like strawberries, and bananas, as well as peanut butter, to thicken the shakes with no chemicals.

6. Maintain a Proper Posture

Patients with dysphagia must consume food and liquids while sitting entirely upright. This makes it easier for food and water to be properly absorbed. You might have to modify the backrest or help the elderly person keep their head and upper body erect while drinking and eating if they are in a wheelchair, hospital bed, or recliner.

7. Pay Attention to Timing

Extreme weariness and weakness may make swallowing for over fifteen minutes at a time for persons with dysphagia signs that come along with chronic diseases like MS or Parkinson's. Your elderly relative will experience a tougher problem properly swallowing meals and liquids the more exhausted they are. A speech therapist could advise that they consume food and liquids periodically throughout the day in small doses. When a senior parent or other older adult is diagnosed with dysphagia, caregiving becomes much more challenging, particularly if the person receiving care also has other long-term medical conditions. If you are concerned about any swallowing issues or if you see any dysphagia signs, consult a doctor straight away.

1.10 Support as a Caregiver

As a caregiver, you might wonder what are the most important things for dysphagia patients. Here I have listed the things that will help you support your loved ones.

1. Maintain Optimal Hydration and Nutrition

It may be challenging for many individuals with dysphagia to keep hydrated, consume enough calories, and get the necessary amounts of minerals and vitamins.

A customized dysphagia diet should be created in consultation with a language pathologist, nutritionist, or other healthcare experts with experience treating swallowing issues to ensure that the person you love maintains sufficient nutrition and hydration. In such adapted diets, thicker meals and beverages are often used since they are safer and simpler for individuals to chew and swallow.

Although not all patients are the same, several meals, like yogurt as well as smoothies, soft fruits, meatloaf, soups, applesauce, and cooked veggies, may be simpler for relatives to take in and prevent dehydration. On the other hand, those who have trouble swallowing should avoid meals like tough meats, peanut butter, and even crusty bread.

Your loved one's liquid intake may rise, and dehydration may be avoided if you give them thickened drinks that appear and taste natural. Besides having access to water that may be sweetened to the patient's preference, beverages that are ready to drink provide those suffering from dysphagia with a range of enticing beverage alternatives, including tea, coffee, and juices.

2. Encourage Proper Swallowing and Eating Skills

The following advice will help you maximize the amount of food consumed and ensure security for your loved one at mealtimes, even if dysphagia can raise the danger of aspiration:

» By giving the person you love a strong chair that enables them to relax securely with both feet on the floor, you may ensure that they are sitting upright when they are eating or drinking.

- » Switching between nibbles and sips can help your relative eat more gently and avoid aspiration. Smaller bites might offer the person you love greater control and decrease the likelihood that the meal will be swallowed before being chewed thoroughly.
- » Before taking the following mouthful, be sure you've finished all your meals and drinks. Ensure that there isn't any food buildup in the cheek or tongue spaces by checking the mouth.
- » Check that the person's dentures are fresh and properly fitted before feeding them, and make sure they practice excellent dental hygiene during the day. One of the major risk factors for aspiration pneumonia, an easily fatal bacterial infection, in people with dysphagia, is poor dental health.

3. Improve Living Quality

Many dysphagia sufferers need to eat carefully and cautiously, tilt or spin the head in a particular direction when swallowing, and adjust their dietary habits by changing to soft or liquid meals to avoid aspiration. Many individuals avoid dining with close companions and quit eating at restaurants if times of eating become a hardship, which causes social isolation and sadness.

You can foster your loved one's pride and feeling of independence as their caretaker. Their self-esteem may be improved by getting them involved in preparing meals and grocery shopping. By providing adapted eating equipment, such as dishes with broad rims, glasses with lids plus wide bases, and non-slip tablecloths to prevent dishes from sliding about the table, you may support the person's independence while they are eating. Allow the person you love to take an active role in the family dinner ritual by allowing them to assist with the kitchen cleanup if they're capable. Ensure that the family member is accommodated before going out to dine or visit a social event by contacting the host family or restaurant in advance. Preparing for a pleasant excursion might make you, as well as your loved one, feel less stressed and anxious.

4. Home Cures and Way of Life

You may also try the following to help your symptoms get better:

- » Modifying your dietary routine. Consider taking shorter, more frequent portions. Eat slowly, properly chew your meal, and cut it up into tiny pieces. There are items available to thicken drinks when you have trouble swallowing liquids.
- » Experiment with various food textures to find which ones make you feel more uncomfortable. Some individuals have trouble swallowing thin liquids like coffee and juice, or sticky foods like peanut butter and caramel may also be problematic. Eat less of the foods that make you sick.

» Limiting coffee and alcohol. These might dry up your tongue and throat, which makes it harder to swallow.

1.11 Ten Strategies for Easier Mealtimes with Dysphagia

During meals, caregivers in the family could get impatient when we wait to take each mouthful or drink. One of the better methods for individuals with more severe dysphagia is feeding with their hands, although it may be very difficult. The following recommendations are made to help with mealtimes and encourage healthy eating practices.

1. Carefully cook and present food, beverages, and snacks according to the dysphagia diet. Utilize an outside thickener or pureed fruit, like prunes and apricots, to thicken drinks. Thickened beverages are far less likely to irritate the throat or lead to aspiration, choking, or coughing than thin liquids. Be aware that particular thicknesses are advised based on one's capacity to swallow and chew.
2. To increase the moisture that helps with swallowing, prepare meals with richer sauces, gravies, or additional toppings.
3. Allow enough time for eating for thorough swallowing and chewing.
4. Remove any distractions from the dining area so that you can fully focus on your food.
5. Encourage others with eye contact and physical indicators like opening and shutting your lips when it's time to bite or drink.
6. Recognize and pay attention to signs of choking, distraction, and food retention in the mouth. Someone who is choking may show signs of being unable to speak, create noise, cough, and inhale.
7. Check that the person you love is chewing food as straight as possible, not slouching or reclining.
8. Choose mealtimes when the person is at their most attentive and cooperative.
9. Consider offering smaller, more manageable servings. Foods that don't need utensils are more easily consumed by certain Alzheimer's sufferers compared to those that do. With the use of finger foods, dementia sufferers may revert to the habitual rhythms and eating motions they have been using their whole lives.
10. Mealtimes demand a lot of persistence, regardless of whether you are assisting a loved one to eat by themselves or not. Allow them plenty of freedom and time as they require to complete their meal. Don't be intrusive; let the individual you love make decisions and respect their decisions. Instead of transient frustration at their delay, let compassion and affection appear on the face.

Chapter 2
Breakfast Recipes

1. Pureed Sausage Gravy and Biscuits

Prep Time: 10 minutes
Cook Time: 10 minutes
Total Time: 20 minutes
Serving: 2
Level: 3

Ingredients:

- Salt and pepper, to taste
- 0.11 lb thawed pureed bulk sausage
- 1 cup prepared country or white gravy

Instructions:

1. Stir 1 cup of prepared country or white gravy into the frozen pureed bulk sausage.
2. Heat, stirring periodically, to 160°F or more.
3. Use salt and pepper to season as required.
4. When serving at 135°F or greater, maintain warm.

Nutrients:

- **Calories:** 120 kcal
- **Total Fats:** 7 g
- **Saturated Fats:** 3.5 g
- **Cholesterol:** 25 mg
- **Sodium:** 440 mg
- **Carbs:** 12 g
- **Fibers:** 0 g
- **Sugar:** 2 g
- **Proteins:** 6 g

2. Pureed Berry Muffins

Prep Time: 10 minutes
Cook Time: 30 minutes
Total Time: 40 minutes
Serving: 1
Level: 4

Ingredients:

- ½ tbsp vegetable oil
- 2 tbsp bread and dessert mix texture-modified
- ½ tsp white sugar
- Pureed-shaped mixed berries
- ½ tbsp smooth seedless, berry jelly or jam
- 2 tbsp hot water

Instructions:

1. Put non-stick cooking spray into muffin cups just enough to coat them.
2. In a bowl, mix white sugar and bread mix. When the mixture looks like wet sand, put oil, then stir.
3. Add boiling water to the bread mixture, then whisk quickly until well combined.
4. Add jelly or jam and gently fold.
5. Place 1 scoop in every muffin cup right away, then distribute evenly using a spatula.
6. For at least 30 minutes, cover and leave the dish at room temperature or in the refrigerator.

7. Take muffin cups out carefully.

Nutrients:
- **Calories:** 150 kcal
- **Total Fats:** 8 g
- **Saturated Fats:** 2 g
- **Cholesterol:** 0 mg
- **Sodium:** 70 mg
- **Carbs:** 22 g
- **Fibers:** 0 g
- **Sugar:** 11 g
- **Proteins:** 2 g

3. Thickened Brown Sugar Milk Tea

Prep Time: 10 minutes
Cook Time: 10 minutes
Total Time: 20 minutes
Serving: 1
Level: 1

Ingredients:
- 6 oz hot water
- 1 stick pack of decaffeinated thickened tea powder
- ¼ cup dairy-thickened drink
- 1–2 tsp brown sugar
- 1–2 tbsp froth or foam from thickened heated dairy drink

Instructions:
1. Brown sugar should be added after adding the decaffeinated thickened tea powder to the bottom of the cup.
2. When the powder is entirely dissolved and the liquid begins to thicken, add boiling water, then stir.
3. Warm up thickened Milk Drink.
4. Stir thoroughly after adding to the thickened tea.
5. If preferred, garnish each dish with 1 to 2 tablespoons of warm dairy drink froth or foam.

Nutrients:
- **Calories:** 100 kcal
- **Total Fats:** 1.5 g
- **Saturated Fats:** 1 g
- **Cholesterol:** 5 mg
- **Sodium:** 85 mg
- **Carbs:** 20 g
- **Fibers:** 0 g
- **Sugar:** 7 g
- **Proteins:** 2 g

4. Apple, Squash, and Turkey Sausage Hash (Moist and Minced)

Prep Time: 15 minutes
Cook Time: 15 minutes
Total Time: 30 minutes
Serving: 2
Level: 4

Ingredients:

- 1 tsp minced, dried onion
- 6 oz raw pork sausage
- 1 cup minced Butternut squash
- 1 cup broth (beef or chicken)
- ¾ cup minced, cored, and peeled apple
- ¼ cup spinach
- 1 ½ tsp instant food thickener
- Salt and pepper, to taste

Instructions:

1. Spray cooking oil on the pan.
2. Cook till meat is brown and no more pink, then stir in sausage and chopped dry onion. Sausage should be broken up into extremely small (1/4" size) crumbs using a spoon/spatula.
3. Take the meat mixture out of the pan and save it.
4. Put broth into the heating pan, boil it, and swirl to remove any bits of meat that may still be stuck to the bottom of the pan.
5. Boil it after adding the chopped butternut squash. For 2 to 3 minutes, decrease the heat, then cover, and simmer.
6. Put the chopped apple, then cover the pot, and boil for a further 3 to 4 minutes, or till the chunks of squash and apple are completely cooked and soft.
7. Stir in the spinach that has been finely chopped.
8. Use salt and pepper to taste to season.
9. Stir the ingredients in the pan after adding a quick food thickener to help any leftover broth become thicker.
10. 135°F maintain hot for serving.

Nutrients:

- **Calories:** 340 kcal
- **Total Fats:** 23 g
- **Saturated Fats:** 8 g
- **Cholesterol:** 60 mg
- **Sodium:** 750 mg
- **Carbs:** 19 g
- **Fibers:** 4 g
- **Sugar:** 8 g
- **Proteins:** 15 g

5. Basted Eggs

Prep Time: 1 minute
Cook Time: 4–5 minutes
Total Time: 5–6 minutes
Serving: 1
Level: 2

Ingredients:

- 1 tbsp very hot water
- 1 egg
- 1 tsp margarine or butter

Instructions:

1. In a pan over moderate temperature, melt butter.
2. Put the egg in.
3. Add water into the skillet once the whites are almost completely set. Close the skillet lid.
4. Cook the egg in the skillet till a thin coating of whites on top of its yolk and the whites around the egg have set.
5. Remove the egg from your skillet and serve.

Nutrients:

- **Calories:** 105 kcal
- **Total Fats:** 8.6 g
- **Saturated Fats:** 1.6 g
- **Cholesterol:** 196 mg
- **Sodium:** 71 mg
- **Carbs:** 0.4 g
- **Fibers:** 0.6 g
- **Sugar:** 0.2 g
- **Proteins:** 6.3 g

6. Coconut Mango Puree

Prep Time: 10 minutes
Cook Time: 0 minutes
Total Time: 10 minutes
Serving: 2
Level: 1

Ingredients:

- 1–2 cans coconut milk
- 1 mango

Instructions:

1. Simply combine 1 ripe mango with 1 to 2 cans of coconut milk in a food processor or blender.
2. You may purchase frozen mango pieces at a grocery store when you do not want to bother with chopping up a mango.
3. If you wish to spice things up a little, add some lime juice to the meal to provide it a nice sour tang.

Nutrients:

- **Calories:** 60 kcal
- **Total Fats:** 0 g
- **Saturated Fats:** 50 g
- **Cholesterol:** 19 mg
- **Sodium:** 50 mg
- **Carbs:** 15 g
- **Fibers:** 2 g
- **Sugar:** 13 g
- **Proteins:** 0.51 g

7. 7. Bread Stuffing

Prep Time: 10 minutes
Cook Time: 10 minutes
Total Time: 20 minutes
Serving: 1
Level: 3

Ingredients:

- ½ tbsp Vegetable oil
- 2 tbsp bread and dessert mix texture-modified
- ⅛ tsp Parsley flakes
- Melted butter or thickened broth, as required
- ⅛ tsp Poultry seasoning scant
- Salt and pepper to taste
- 3 tbsp chicken broth, hot

Instructions:

1. Apply non-stick cooking spray liberally to the pan.
2. Combine bread and dessert mix whose texture is modified, poultry spice, plus parsley. When the mixture

resembles moist sand, put oil, then stir.
3. Put hot broth, salt, and pepper then quickly whisk the mixture until it starts to thicken.
4. The bread mixture may be spooned into muffin cups.
5. For at least 30 minutes, cover and leave the dish at room temperature or inside the refrigerator.

Nutrients:
- **Calories:** 30 kcal
- **Total Fats:** 3 g
- **Saturated Fats:** 1 g
- **Cholesterol:** 0 mg
- **Sodium:** 210 mg
- **Carbs:** 13 g
- **Fibers:** 0 g
- **Sugar:** 3 g
- **Proteins:** 3 g

8. Cranberry Almond Bread

Prep Time: 10 minutes
Cook Time: 5 minutes
Total Time: 15 minutes
Serving: 1
Level: 2

Ingredients:
- ½ tbsp vegetable oil
- 2 tbsp pureed bread and dessert mix
- ⅛ tsp vanilla extract
- 1 ½ tsp thickened orange juice
- ½ tsp brown sugar
- 1 ½ tbsp water
- 1/16 tsp almond extract
- 1 tbsp jellied cranberry sauce

Instructions:
1. Carefully apply non-stick spray on the pan.
2. In a large basin, mix bread mix and brown sugar. When the mixture looks like wet sand, put oil, then stir.
3. To boiling water, add vanilla and almond extracts. Add to the bread mix and quickly toss to combine.
4. Incorporate the liquefied cranberry juice gently.
5. Pour bread into the pan right away.
6. For 30 minutes or till set, cover and let to cool at room temperature or in the refrigerator.
7. Over the bread, brush the orange juice that has been thickened.
8. Each serving should consist of 1 slice of bread or around 1/2 cup.

Nutrients:
- **Calories:** 160 kcal
- **Total Fats:** 8 g
- **Saturated Fats:** 1 g
- **Cholesterol:** 0 mg
- **Sodium:** 75 g
- **Carbs:** 22 g
- **Fibers:** 0 g
- **Sugar:** 10 g
- **Proteins:** 2 g

9. Cranberry Pear Tart

Prep Time: 30 minutes
Cook Time: 15 minutes
Total Time: 34 minutes
Serving: 1
Level: 3

Ingredients:

Crust:

- 1 tbsp cookie or cracker crumbs
- 2 tsp bread and dessert mix
- 1 tsp vegetable oil
- 1 ½ tbsp water
- ⅛ tsp sugar
- 1–2 drops almond extract

Filling:

- ¾ tsp water
- 2 tbsp jellied cranberry
- 1 tsp lemon juice
- ½ tsp brown sugar
- 2 ½ tbsp pears
- ¼ tsp butter
- ½ tsp cornstarch
- 1–2 drops vanilla extract

Instructions:

For Crust:

1. Use a lot of non-stick cooking spray to coat the pan.
2. Bread and dessert mix, cookie crumbs, and sugar should be combined. When the mixture looks like wet sand, put oil and almond essence (if desired), then stir.
3. The mixture of the bread and liquid should be quickly stirred to combine.
4. Add the crust mixture to the pan.
5. Push the crust onto the pan's sides after pressing it flat.
6. Put the crust in the freezer or fridge for a minimum of 2 hours till they are hard.

For Filling:

1. In a small saucepan, mix water and sauce of jellied cranberry. Heat until melted.
2. Stir in the brown sugar till it is dissolved.
3. Mix the cornstarch and lemon juice well in a tiny container.
4. In the pan, stir the dissolved cranberry sauce.
5. Cook till thickened and the mixture starts to boil.
6. Mix in butter and vanilla essence after removing from the heat.
7. Spread the chilled filling equally into the prepared crust after cooling the contents in the refrigerator.
8. Place a layer of cranberry filling over top of the pureed pears. Pear puree

may be formed into forms like pear slices by forcing it through a piping bag. Alternatively, drop the spoonful of pears into the filling, then swirl them to make a pretty pattern. Frozen and pureed-shaped pears should be sliced into pieces after they have been slightly frozen and placed on top of the tart if utilizing them.

9. When ready to serve, cover the completed tart loosely with wrapping paper and place it in the refrigerator or freezer.
10. Cut servings into thirds and garnish using whipped topping.
11. Dessert should be sliced and portioned when frozen for simplicity of serving. Before serving, thaw completely.

Nutrients:

- **Calories:** 180 kcal
- **Total Fats:** 6 g
- **Saturated Fats:** 1 g
- **Cholesterol:** 0 mg
- **Sodium:** 75 mg
- **Carbs:** 29 g
- **Fibers:** 0 g
- **Sugar:** 2 g
- **Proteins:** 1 g

10. Pureed Broccoli, Cheese, and Egg Dish

Prep Time: 20 minutes
Cook Time: 15 minutes
Total Time: 35 minutes
Serving: 1
Level: 3

Ingredients:

- 2 tsp milk
- 1 egg scrambled eggs, prepared
- A dash salt
- ½ tsp instant food thickener
- A dash dry mustard
- A dash black pepper
- 1/3 cup broccoli
- 2 tsp cheese, finely shredded
- 2 tsp water or broth
- Cheese sauce as required
- ¾ tsp instant food thickener
- ¼ tsp margarine or butter

Instructions:

1. Spray non-stick cooking spray on the pan.
2. Blend or process milk and scrambled eggs till completely smooth.
3. Add the initial quantity of cheese along with the pepper, salt, dry mustard, plus instant food and beverage thickener. Just long enough for the ingredients to be well combined.
4. Scoop portions of the egg mixture at random into the pan. Place aside.
5. Blend broccoli and water until completely smooth. Add the second quantity of cheese along with instant food and beverage thickener. Just long enough for the ingredients to be well combined.

6. Place the broccoli mixture on the pan next to the egg at random intervals. Spread uniformly.
7. To gently mix the 2 ingredients, put a flat spatula in the pan and draw through puree multiple times.
8. Bake at 350°F till the internal temperature hits 165°F, then securely cover with aluminum foil.

Nutrients:
- **Calories:** 170 kcal
- **Total Fats:** 11 g
- **Saturated Fats:** 4.5 g
- **Cholesterol:** 180 mg
- **Sodium:** 370 mg
- **Carbs:** 7 g
- **Fibers:** 2 g
- **Sugar:** 0 g
- **Proteins:** 11 g

11. Chocolate Avocado Pudding

Prep Time: 30 minutes
Cook Time: 0 minutes
Total Time: 30 minutes
Serving: 2
Level: 1

Ingredients:
- ½ cup cocoa powder
- 2 ripe avocados
- 1 pinch cinnamon, grounded
- ½ cup brown sugar
- 2 tsp vanilla extract
- ½ cup coconut milk

Instructions:
1. Blend the following ingredients in a blender: cocoa powder, avocados, coconut milk, brown sugar, vanilla essence, and cinnamon.
2. The pudding should be refrigerated in the refrigerator for approximately 30 minutes.

Nutrients:
- **Calories:** 87 kcal
- **Total Fats:** 7 g
- **Saturated Fats:** 1 g
- **Cholesterol:** 0 mg
- **Sodium:** 10 mg
- **Carbs:** 9 g
- **Fibers:** 3.2 g
- **Sugar:** 1.7 g
- **Proteins:** 1.5 g

12. Apple Crumble

Prep Time: 15 minutes
Cook Time: 12 minutes
Total Time: 27 minutes
Serving: 1
Level: 2

Ingredients:

- 1 tsp cinnamon
- Two tubs of apple puree (that weighs 0.24-lb each), unsweetened
- ¾ cup water
- Extra cinnamon and brown sugar
- ½ cup quick oats

Instructions:

1. Set oven to 390°F.
2. An oven-safe bowl should be filled with water and oats. One minute on high in the microwave. Stir. Once again, heat for fifty seconds. Cool after removing from microwave. Mix in a food processor for 1 minute on high after transferring.
3. Put 2 ramekins with apple purée inside. Each ramekin should have 1/2 teaspoon of cinnamon.
4. Add 2 tablespoons of the oat mix to the apple. Add as much cinnamon and brown sugar as you want.
5. For 8 to 10 minutes, bake.
6. If preferred, sprinkle with cinnamon and brown sugar before serving.

Nutrients:

- **Calories:** 227 kcal
- **Total Fats:** 4.8 g
- **Saturated Fats:** 1 g
- **Cholesterol:** 0 mg
- **Sodium:** 495 mg
- **Carbs:** 43 g
- **Fibers:** 7 g
- **Sugar:** 28 g
- **Proteins:** 2.5 g

13. Baked Custard

Prep Time: 15 minutes
Cook Time: 60 minutes
Total Time: 75 minutes
Serving: 3
Level: 2

Ingredients:

- 3 whole eggs
- 2 tbsp sugar
- 1 tsp vanilla
- 2 ½ cups milk
- Cinnamon or nutmeg, as needed
- Water, as needed

Instructions:

1. Set the oven's temperature to 320°F.
2. Eggs, vanilla, and sugar are softly whipped together.
3. Before adding milk slowly to the egg mix while continually stirring, gently warm it on the burner.

4. Sprinkle cinnamon and/or nutmeg over the mixture after pouring it into a small ovenproof dish.
5. Put the plate in a bath of water with water that reaches halfway to the dish's edges.
6. Cook for 30 minutes in the oven, then continue baking for an additional 20 to 30 minutes at 280°F until the mixture is set.

Nutrients:
- **Calories:** 80 kcal
- **Total Fats:** 2.5 g
- **Saturated Fats:** 1.2 g
- **Cholesterol:** 67 mg
- **Sodium:** 157 mg
- **Carbs:** 12 g
- **Fibers:** 0 g
- **Sugar:** 8.3 g
- **Proteins:** 4.6 g

14. Maple Sweet Carrot Puree

Prep Time: 10 minutes
Cook Time: 5 minutes
Total Time: 15 minutes
Serving: 1
Level: 1

Ingredients:
- ⅛ cup butter
- Salt to taste
- 5 cups fresh carrots
- ¼ cup maple syrup
- 1 cup water

Instructions:
1. Carrots should be boiled in 1 cup of salted water with the lid on.
2. Simmer over a medium-low flame till it is fork-tender.
3. Strain carrots.
4. Warm carrots are combined with butter and maple syrup, then blended until creamy.

Nutrients:
- **Calories:** 211 kcal
- **Total Fats:** 14 g
- **Saturated Fats:** 2 g
- **Cholesterol:** 12 mg
- **Sodium:** 108 mg
- **Carbs:** 21 g
- **Fibers:** 4 g
- **Sugar:** 13 g
- **Proteins:** 2 g

15. Pumpkin Brownie Puree

Prep Time: 15 minutes
Cook Time: 25 minutes
Total Time: 40 minutes
Serving: 4
Level: 3

Ingredients:

- ¼ cup pumpkin puree
- 12 tsp milk
- 1 box brownie mix

Instructions:

1. Heat at 350°F the oven.
2. Oil a 9x9-inch pan.
3. Blend brownie mix and pumpkin puree till thoroughly combined in a bowl.
4. Pour onto a prepared pan, then bake for 20 to 25 minutes.
5. Let the brownies cool.
6. The blender should be filled with the required quantity of brownies. Blend in the milk, 1 tablespoon at a time, until the mixture is smooth.
7. Add some more brownie, then mix to thicken if the brownie is too runny.

Nutrients:

- **Calories:** 135 kcal
- **Total Fats:** 2.7 g
- **Saturated Fats:** 0.8 g
- **Cholesterol:** 0 mg
- **Sodium:** 278 mg
- **Carbs:** 26.6 g
- **Fibers:** 1.4 g
- **Sugar:** 14 g
- **Proteins:** 1.8 g

16. Peach Apricot Puree

Prep Time: 10 minutes
Cook Time: 5 minutes
Total Time: 15 minutes
Serving: 2
Level: 1

Ingredients:

- 0.5 lb dried apricots
- 2 lb frozen peaches
- 1 tbsp cinnamon
- ⅔ cup quick 1-minute oats
- 2 cups apple juice

Instructions:

1. Pour apple juice, frozen peaches, cinnamon, and apricots into the saucepan.
2. Increase the heat until the mixture begins to boil.
3. Five minutes at a high temperature, stirring periodically.
4. Oats are added, well mixed, and the water is then brought back to a boil.
5. Blend the ingredients of the pot.
6. Blend fully until smooth (1 to 3 minutes).

Nutrients:

- **Calories:** 43 kcal
- **Total Fats:** 0.08 g
- **Saturated Fats:** 0 g
- **Cholesterol:** 0 mg
- **Sodium:** 2.27 g
- **Carbs:** 11 g
- **Fibers:** 1.2 g
- **Sugar:** 2 g
- **Proteins:** 0.71 g

17. Fig Berry Puree

Prep Time: 15 minutes
Cook Time: 10 minutes
Total Time: 25 minutes
Serving: 1
Level: 1

Ingredients:

- 0.5 lb dried figs
- 2 lb frozen strawberries
- 1 tsp ground cloves
- 1 cup quick, 1-minute oats
- 1 cup apple juice

Instructions:

1. Remove any stems that remain at the pointy tip of your figs after cutting them in half.
2. If preparing fresh strawberries, split them in half and discard their top and bottom.
3. In a saucepan, combine the figs, strawberries, and apple juice.
4. Increase the heat, then cover.
5. Boil for 5 minutes, stirring once the water begins to boil.
6. Oats are added, stirred, and let 1 more minute to boil.
7. Once the pan has been taken off the heat, transfer the contents and the crushed cloves into a blender. Never load your blender more than halfway; else, heated food may shoot out the top. A towel should be placed on top for further protection, and a lid should be tight.
8. Mix until uniform (2 to 3 minutes).

Nutrients:

- **Calories:** 25 kcal
- **Total Fats:** 0 g
- **Saturated Fats:** 0 g
- **Cholesterol:** 0 mg
- **Sodium:** 0 g
- **Carbs:** 6 g
- **Fibers:** 0 g
- **Sugar:** 1 g
- **Proteins:** 1 g

18. Peaches and Cream

Prep Time: 5 minutes
Cook Time: 0 minutes
Total Time: 5 minutes
Serving: 1
Level: 1

Ingredients:

- ⅛ tsp vanilla extract
- 1 cup ice cream
- 1 jar baby peaches
- A pinch nutmeg

Instructions:

1. One baby peach jar should be strained.
2. Put ⅛ teaspoon of vanilla essence, ⅛ teaspoon of nutmeg, and 1 cup of ice cream.
3. Until smooth, blend.

Nutrients:

- **Calories:** 140 kcal
- **Total Fats:** 2 g
- **Saturated Fats:** 0.5 g
- **Cholesterol:** 0 mg
- **Sodium:** 140 mg
- **Carbs:** 27 g
- **Fibers:** 2 g
- **Sugar:** 11 g
- **Proteins:** 3 g

19. Frozen Yogurt Parfait

Prep Time: 5 minutes
Cook Time: 0 minutes
Total Time: 5 minutes
Serving: 1
Level: 1

Ingredients:

- Almond milk a small amount
- Favorite fruits as required
- Vanilla yogurt as required

Instructions:

1. Your elderly citizens' favorite fruits, some almond milk, plus vanilla yogurt should all be blended.
2. Serve right now or freeze for an overnight treat that tastes and is healthful, like ice cream.

Nutrients:
- **Calories:** 320 kcal
- **Total Fats:** 4.5 g
- **Saturated Fats:** 0 g
- **Cholesterol:** 0 mg
- **Sodium:** 150 mg
- **Carbs:** 67 g
- **Fibers:** 5 g
- **Sugar:** 47 g
- **Proteins:** 6 g

20. Scrambled Egg and Bean Puree

Prep Time: 10 minutes
Cook Time: 10 minutes
Total Time: 20 minutes
Serving: 1
Level: 3

Ingredients:
- Salt and pepper to taste
- 1 egg
- 2 tbsp broth
- 3 tbsp enchilada sauce
- ½ cup black beans

Instructions:
1. On medium heat, sauté the beans and the sauce for enchilada in a skillet.
2. Add your preferred broth after around 2 minutes.
3. Mix the mixture using a handheld blender or a standard blender, then pour it into a serving dish.
4. Another option is to prepare the bean puree ahead of time and store it in the refrigerator while you prepare the eggs.
5. Before placing the eggs in a heated pan, mix them inside a basin first.
6. Take care to stir the eggs using a spatula while they cook and season with pepper and salt to taste.
7. Take them out from the fire once they have the right consistency, then serve them alongside bean puree and enchilada sauce.

Nutrients:
- **Calories:** 479 kcal
- **Total Fats:** 23 g
- **Saturated Fats:** 8 g
- **Cholesterol:** 395 mg
- **Sodium:** 1291 mg
- **Carbs:** 44 g
- **Fibers:** 11 g
- **Sugar:** 2 g
- **Proteins:** 23 g

21. Pureed Egg Salad

Prep Time: 5 minutes
Cook Time: 0 minutes
Total Time: 5 minutes
Serving: 1
Level: 1

Ingredients:

- 1–½ tbsp chopped green onion
- 2 hard-boiled eggs
- 2 tbsp cheese cottage
- 2 tbsp diced tomatoes
- Salt and pepper to taste
- 2 tsp reduced-fat mayonnaise
- 1 tsp olives sliced

Instructions:

1. Combine all ingredients—except the cheese—in a bowl.
2. Blend the ingredients in a blender or food processor until they have a creamy texture.
3. Add the cheese gradually, and then serve cold.

Nutrients:

- **Calories:** 199 kcal
- **Total Fats:** 14 g
- **Saturated Fats:** 3 g
- **Cholesterol:** 39 mg
- **Sodium:** 220 mg
- **Carbs:** 3 g
- **Fibers:** 0 g
- **Sugar:** 2 g
- **Proteins:** 13 g

22. Scrambled Eggs

Prep Time: 5 minutes
Cook Time: 5 minutes
Total Time: 10 minutes
Serving: 1
Level: 3

Ingredients:

- 0.18 lb milk
- Pepper and salt to taste
- 2 eggs

Instructions:

1. In a bowl, combine 1 ounce of milk, salt, 2 eggs, and pepper.
2. In a large skillet over medium to low heat, scramble the eggs.
3. While preparing, stir often to prevent overcooking.
4. Add 2 more ounces of milk to the mixture inside a blender or food processor, and pulse until smooth.

Nutrients:

- **Calories:** 91 kcal
- **Total Fats:** 6.7 g
- **Saturated Fats:** 2 g
- **Cholesterol:** 169 mg
- **Sodium:** 88 mg
- **Carbs:** 1 g
- **Fibers:** 0 g
- **Sugar:** 0 g
- **Proteins:** 6.1 g

Chapter 3
Lunch Recipes

1. Fresh Pea Soup

Prep Time: 10 minutes
Cook Time: 5 minutes
Total Time: 15 minutes
Serving: 2
Level: 1

Ingredients:

- 2 ½ cups chicken broth
- 1 cup peas
- A pinch ginger
- 1 tbsp butter
- 1 tbsp diced onion
- A pinch pepper
- 2 tsp flour

Instructions:

1. In a saucepan, combine onions, peas, and chicken broth.
2. Cook over a medium-high flame for the veggies to become soft.
3. Once the veggies are completely melted, mix in butter, ginger, and pepper.
4. Mix the ingredients well in the blender or mixer after adding them.
5. Put the thickening agent into the combined mixture before transferring it back to the saucepan.
6. The soup should be heated through before simmering for 5 minutes.

Nutrients:

- **Calories:** 158 kcal
- **Total Fats:** 2.8 g
- **Saturated Fats:** 1.4 g
- **Cholesterol:** 0 mg
- **Sodium:** 870 mg
- **Carbs:** 26 g
- **Fibers:** 4.9 g
- **Sugar:** 8.3 g
- **Proteins:** 8.3 g

2. Lima Bean Purée

Prep Time: 20 minutes
Cook Time: 45 minutes
Total Time: 65 minutes
Serving: 2
Level: 1

Ingredients:

- 3 cups vegetable or water broth
- 1 tsp olive oil
- 0.5 lb dry lima beans
- ½ tsp salt

Instructions:

1. By eliminating ruined beans and stones, the beans are sorted. Drain the beans after washing them in cool water.
2. In a pot with salt and water, cook the beans.
3. Low heat is applied while the pan is covered. The beans should be quite soft after 45 minutes of boiling.

4. The beans should be added to a blender. It should yield roughly 3 cups when the liquid is included.
5. Oil should be added, and after 20 to 30 seconds, the beans should be extremely smooth.

Nutrients:
- **Calories:** 209 kcal
- **Total Fats:** 0.5 g
- **Saturated Fats:** 0 g
- **Cholesterol:** 0 mg
- **Sodium:** 28.9 mg
- **Carbs:** 40 g
- **Fibers:** 9.2 g
- **Sugar:** 2.8 g
- **Proteins:** 11.6 g

3. Pumpkin Cauliflower Curry

Prep Time: 10 minutes
Cook Time: 10 minutes
Total Time: 20 minutes
Serving: 1
Level: 1

Ingredients:
- 0.5 lb pumpkin
- 0.5 lb cauliflower
- 1 tbsp olive oil
- 1 tbsp. greek yogurt
- 1 cup water
- A dash pepper
- 1 tbsp curry powder

Instructions:
1. Cauliflower and pumpkin should first be chopped into tiny bits.
2. Curry paste is added to a wok that has been heated with oil.
3. The combination is stirred until it is aromatic. Mix it for 2 minutes after adding the pumpkin.
4. Put the water after that, and allow it to boil. Continually whisk the mixture while it boils for 5 minutes.
5. After that, add the cauliflower and bring the water to a boil. For 2 minutes, allow it to simmer.
6. Yogurt is optional, so add it now and cook for 2 more minutes.
7. Following that, add a pinch of ground pepper to the blender along with your curry. The curry must be thoroughly smooth after blending.

Nutrients:
- **Calories:** 418 kcal
- **Total Fats:** 19 g
- **Saturated Fats:** 7.6 g
- **Cholesterol:** 0 mg
- **Sodium:** 0 g
- **Carbs:** 70 g
- **Fibers:** 12 g
- **Sugar:** 22 g
- **Proteins:** g

4. Chili

Prep Time: 10 minutes
Cook Time: 15–20 minutes
Total Time: 25–30 minutes
Serving: 6
Level: 2

Ingredients:

- 1 ½ cup onion
- 2 tbsp olive oil
- 1 tbsp garlic, minced
- 2 tbsp chili powder
- 1 ½ tsp oregano
- 1 tsp cumin
- 1 tsp salt
- 1 tsp dry ground mustard
- 1 cup packet of beef bouillon
- ½ tsp black pepper
- 8 oz tomato sauce
- 1 (1 lb) can crushed tomatoes canned
- Chopped green onions, as much as you need 1 (¾ lb) bag ground minced beef
- Sour cream, as required
- 1 (1 lb) can refried beans

Instructions:

1. With olive oil, cook finely sliced onions until they become transparent.
2. Add the cumin, chili powder, salt, mustard, and pepper, along with the chopped garlic and oregano.
3. Stir thoroughly after adding crushed tomatoes, tomato sauce, and beef broth.
4. For 8 to 10 minutes, cover and simmer.
5. Add frozen minced beef along with refried beans.
6. Simmer the chili for a further 3 to 5 minutes.
7. 1 cup should be allotted in each serving.
8. As desired, top extra sour cream and coarsely sliced green onion.

Nutrients:

- **Calories:** 280 kcal
- **Total Fats:** 13 g
- **Saturated Fats:** 3.5 g
- **Cholesterol:** 55 mg
- **Sodium:** 1.1 g
- **Carbs:** 24 g
- **Fibers:** 7 g
- **Sugar:** 7 g
- **Proteins:** 20 g

5. Chicken a la King

Prep Time: 15 minutes
Cook Time: 20 minutes
Total Time: 35 minutes
Serving: 6
Level: 4

Ingredients:

- 1 ½ oz sliced fresh mushroom
- 2 tsp butter
- 5 tbsp butter
- ¼ cup onions, diced
- ¼ cup flour
- 1 cup milk
- 1 ½ cup chicken broth
- ¼ tsp black pepper
- ½ tsp salt
- 3 cups bulk pureed rice
- 6 tbsp bulk pureed peas
- 1 ½ cup ground minced chicken
- 1 ½ tsp finely diced pimento

Instructions:

1. In the initial quantity of butter, sauté mushrooms and onions until they are soft. Take out of the pan, then purée inside a food processor. Place aside.
2. Melt more butter inside a saucepan. Until the mixture is smooth, add the flour and beat with the help of a wire whisk.
3. Whisk in the milk and chicken broth till combined.
4. Bring ingredients to boil while stirring continuously until thickened.
5. Add pepper, salt, and frozen ground chicken, along with the ground mushrooms and onions. Stir and cook until food reaches a temperature of 165°F.

Nutrients:

- **Calories:** 380 kcal
- **Total Fats:** 25 g
- **Saturated Fats:** 10 g
- **Cholesterol:** 65 mg
- **Sodium:** 980 mg
- **Carbs:** 24 g
- **Fibers:** 1 g
- **Sugar:** 4 g
- **Proteins:** 13 g

6. Turkey Tetrazzini

Prep Time: 15 minutes
Cook Time: 20 minutes
Total Time: 35 minutes
Serving: 2
Level: 4

Ingredients:

- ½ cup bulk-pureed pasta
- ¼ cup creamy mushroom or tetrazzini sauce
- ½ cup ground turkey

Instructions:

1. Combine ground Turkey. Prepare a smooth sauce and thoroughly whisk it.
2. Heat thoroughly until the inside reaches 165°F.
3. Keep at 135°F or greater to keep warm for service.
4. Prepare bulk pureed pasta and hold until serving.
5. Add roughly ⅔ cup of the turkey and sauce combination to the pasta.
6. If desired, add shredded Parmesan cheese as a garnish.

Nutrients:

- **Calories:** 360 kcal
- **Total Fats:** 23 g
- **Saturated Fats:** 8 g
- **Cholesterol:** 90 mg
- **Sodium:** 640 mg
- **Carbs:** 18 g
- **Fibers:** 2 g
- **Sugar:** 1 g
- **Proteins:** 18 g

7. Pureed Pasta with Beef Marinara

Prep Time: 10 minutes
Cook Time: 20 minutes
Total Time: 30 minutes
Serving: 1
Level: 3

Ingredients:

- ¼ cup red sauce
- Food thickener, as needed
- ½ cup ground beef, thawed
- ½ cup bulk thickened pureed pasta blend

Instructions:

1. Red sauce, food thickener, and ground beef should be well mixed.
2. Cook well until the internal temperature reaches 165°F.
3. Keep at 135°F or greater to maintain warm for service.
4. Prepare bulk pureed thickening pasta blend, then keep until serving.
5. Place ½ cup of spaghetti purée onto a dish to serve.
6. Add roughly ⅔ cup of the meat and sauce combination to the pasta.
7. If preferred, garnish using finely chopped parsley and Parmesan cheese.

Nutrients:

- **Calories:** 320 kcal
- **Total Fats:** 19 g
- **Saturated Fats:** 4.5 g
- **Cholesterol:** 55 mg
- **Sodium:** 630 mg
- **Carbs:** 21 g
- **Fibers:** 1 g
- **Sugar:** 5 g
- **Proteins:** 17 g

8. Vegetable Fried Rice

Prep Time: 20 minutes
Cook Time: 10 minutes
Total Time: 30 minutes
Serving: 1
Level: 3

Ingredients:

- 1 tsp soy sauce
- ½ cup pureed rice, thawed
- ⅛ tsp black pepper
- ¼ tsp toasted sesame oil
- ¼ tsp onion powder
- Soy sauce for garnish
- ½ oz shaped-pureed carrots portion
- ⅛ tsp garlic powder
- ½ oz shaped-pureed peas portion

Instructions:

1. As directed on the packaging, heat pureed rice to 165°F.
2. Stir thoroughly after adding the soy sauce, onion, toasted sesame oil, garlic, and pepper. For serving, hold around 135°F or above.
3. As directed on the packaging, preheat the pureed-shaped carrot and pea to 165°F. Garnish with soy sauce.

Nutrients:

- **Calories:** 220 kcal
- **Total Fats:** 14 g
- **Saturated Fats:** 3 g
- **Cholesterol:** 30 mg
- **Sodium:** 750 mg
- **Carbs:** 20 g
- **Fibers:** 1 g
- **Sugar:** 4 g
- **Proteins:** 4 g

9. Hamburger and Bun

Prep Time: 25 minutes
Cook Time: 20 minutes
Total Time: 45 minutes
Serving: 1
Level: 4

Ingredients:

Burger:

- ½ cup minced beef
- 1 ½ tsp food and beverage thickener
- 3 tbsp water or beef broth

Bun:
- » 3 tbsp water
- » ½ tbsp vegetable oil
- » 2 tbsp bread and dessert mix texture-modified

Instructions:

For Burger Patties:
1. Add hot broth or water to the instant food and beverage thickener and whisk vigorously till the mixture begins to thicken.
2. Stir the ingredient into the minced beef once it has thawed.
3. To give the meat mixture more taste, herbs or spices may be added as needed.
4. At 135°F or above, cover and hold for serving.

For Bun:
1. The bread mix should look like wet sand after you've added the vegetable oil and stirred it.
2. The mixture of the bread and liquid should be quickly stirred to combine.
3. Scoop portions of the bread mixture on a baking sheet covered with parchment or wax paper.
4. For a minimum of 30 minutes, cover using plastic wrap and let the food rest at room temperature.

To Serve:
1. Every bread scoop should be flattened and shaped into 2 to 3-inch circles with a clean, gloved palm.
2. On the serving dish, place 1 bread circle.
3. Add a thin layer of thickened beef mixture over top, roughly 2 ounces, and spread with a spatula.
4. Add your preferred burger toppings.
5. On the surface of the meat patty, put the bread circle.

Nutrients:
- » **Calories:** 240 kcal
- » **Total Fats:** 14 g
- » **Saturated Fats:** 4 g
- » **Cholesterol:** 55 mg
- » **Sodium:** 250 mg
- » **Carbs:** 15 g
- » **Fibers:** 0 g
- » **Sugar:** 3 g
- » **Proteins:** 16 g

10. PUREED CORNBREAD

Prep Time: 10 minutes
Cook Time: 10 minutes
Total Time: 20 minutes
Serving: 1
Level: 2

Ingredients:
- » ½ cup water
- » 1 tbsp cornmeal
- » ¼ cup water
- » ¼ tsp sugar
- » 2 tbsp bread and dessert mix texture-modified
- » 1 tsp butter

Instructions:

1. Bring half of the water to a boil after dividing it.
2. Add the cornmeal to the second half of the water and mix well before adding to the boiling water.
3. Stirring periodically, bring the liquid to a boil, then simmer until the cornmeal has softened and the sauce is thick.
4. Place aside and let it cool.
5. Pureed bread and dessert together. Stir the mixture while adding water till it starts to thicken.
6. Stir together the bread and cooked cornmeal. Stir in the butter and sugar. Before serving, distribute or portion the food into the pans and let it cool, then set it for 10 minutes.
7. If preferred, top with honey or melted butter while serving.

Nutrients:

- **Calories:** 130 kcal
- **Total Fats:** 5 g
- **Saturated Fats:** 3 g
- **Cholesterol:** 10 mg
- **Sodium:** 135 mg
- **Carbs:** 18 g
- **Fibers:** 1 g
- **Sugar:** 4 g
- **Proteins:** 3 g

11. BEEF STROGANOFF

Prep Time: 15 minutes
Cook Time: 20 minutes
Total Time: 30 minutes
Serving: 6
Level: 4

Ingredients:

- 3 oz fresh sliced mushroom
- 1 tbsp butter
- ½ cup onions, diced
- 1 tsp Worcestershire sauce
- ½ tsp garlic, minced
- 1 tbsp butter
- 3 cups bulk pureed pasta
- 1 ½ cup beef broth
- 2 tbsp flour
- ½ tsp salt
- ½ cup sour cream
- ¼ tsp black pepper
- 1 ½ cup ground minced beef

Instructions:

1. In the initial quantity of butter, add onions and sauté mushrooms until they are soft. After 1 minute or 2, add the garlic.
2. Take out of pan and purée or ground in a blender. Place aside.
3. Melt more butter inside a saucepan. Add the flour and whisk using a wire till it is completely dissolved.
4. Whisk in the beef broth and Worcestershire sauce till combined.
5. Bring ingredients to a boil while stirring continuously until thickened.
6. Stir in the sour cream, salt, and pepper.
7. Put ground mushrooms, ground onions, and thawed ground beef. Stir frequently until food reaches a temperature of 165°F.

Nutrients:
- **Calories:** 320 kcal
- **Total Fats:** 22 g
- **Saturated Fats:** 7 g
- **Cholesterol:** 45 mg
- **Sodium:** 790 mg
- **Carbs:** 20g
- **Fibers:** 0 g
- **Sugar:** 3 g
- **Proteins:** 11 g

12. MINCED TURKEY TETRAZZINI

Prep Time: 15 minutes
Cook Time: 20 minutes
Total Time: 35 minutes
Serving: 2
Level: 3

Ingredients:
- ½ cup bulk pureed pasta
- ¼ cup creamy mushroom or tetrazzini sauce
- ½ cup ground minced turkey

Instructions:
1. Mix minced turkey. Prepare a smooth sauce, then thoroughly whisk it.
2. Heat thoroughly until the inside reaches 165°F.
3. Keep at 135°F or greater to keep warm for service.
4. Follow the instructions and prepare bulk pureed pasta, and hold until serving.
5. Add roughly ⅔ cup of the turkey and sauce combination to the pasta.
6. If desired, add shredded Parmesan cheese as a garnish.

Nutrients:
- **Calories:** 360 kcal
- **Total Fats:** 23 g
- **Saturated Fats:** 8 g
- **Cholesterol:** 90 mg
- **Sodium:** 640 mg
- **Carbs:** 18 g
- **Fibers:** 2 g
- **Sugar:** 2 g
- **Proteins:** 18 g

13. CORNED BEEF AND CABBAGE

Prep Time: 15 minutes
Cook Time: 10–20 minutes
Total Time: 25–35 minutes
Serving: 1
Level: 4

Ingredients:
- ¼ cup beef broth low sodium
- 3 oz corned beef
- ½ cup cabbage, cooked
- 1 tbsp mustard sauce
- ½ tbsp food thickener
- 1 tbsp food thickener
- 1 ½ tsp broth, low sodium

Instructions:

1. In a food processor or blender, puree the corned beef using heated broth until the consistency is smooth.
2. Incorporate food thickener after adding it.
3. Spread into the skillet or pan with frying spray.
4. When the temperature hits 165°F and a knife inserted in the middle of the pan pulls out clean, cover the pan securely with foil, then bake this at 350°F or cook using a steamer.
5. Puree the cooked cabbage inside a blender till smooth.
6. Add the required quantity of the liquid that was set aside and blend until smooth.
7. Add the remaining food thickener, then blend just long enough to mix.
8. Spread into the skillet or pans with frying spray.
9. When the temperature hits 165°F and a knife put in the middle of the pan pulls out clean, cover the pan securely with foil, then bake at 350°F or cook inside a steamer.
10. Before cutting and dividing it into the necessary number of portions, let it stand for about 5 minutes.
11. Put 1 slice of the pureed corned beef, 1 scoop, or 1 formed and molded slice onto the serving platter.
12. Each dish should include 1 scoop of cabbage.
13. If preferred, top each meal with 1 tablespoon of mustard sauce.

Nutrients:

- **Calories:** 280 kcal
- **Total Fats:** 16 g
- **Saturated Fats:** 5 g
- **Cholesterol:** 85 mg
- **Sodium:** 1.0 g
- **Carbs:** 14 g
- **Fibers:** 1 g
- **Sugar:** 14 g
- **Proteins:** 19 g

14. White Sauce Pasta Recipe

Prep Time: 5 minutes
Cook Time: 10 minutes
Total Time: 15 minutes
Serving: 6
Level: 4

Ingredients:

- 3 tbsp unsalted butter
- 1 package penne
- 3 tbsp flour all-purpose
- 2 tsp minced garlic
- 1 cup milk
- 1 cup Parmesan cheese, grated
- 1 cup chicken broth
- ½ cup mozzarella cheese, shredded
- 2 tsp dried parsley
- Pepper to taste
- Garlic salt to taste

Instructions:

1. As directed on the box, cook the noodles, drain, and then put them apart.

2. Meanwhile, soften butter inside a sizable skillet over a moderate flame. Add the garlic and sauté for 1 minute.
3. Cook for about an additional minute while continuously tossing in the flour.
4. Cook, whisking continuously, till sauce boils as well as thickens, for 5 minutes after adding the milk and stock.
5. Pepper, garlic, salt, and herbs should also be added.
6. Stir the noodles into the liquid to incorporate. Melt the cheese by adding it and stirring. Serve hot.

Nutrients:
- **Calories:** 191 kcal
- **Total Fats:** 7.3 g
- **Saturated Fats:** 4.4 g
- **Cholesterol:** 20 mg
- **Sodium:** 88 mg
- **Carbs:** 10 g
- **Fibers:** 0.5 g
- **Sugar:** 0.4 g
- **Proteins:** 2.8 g

15. Pureed Lemon Cream Cheese Pie

Prep Time: 20 minutes
Cook Time: 20 minutes
Total Time: 40 minutes
Serving: 1
Level: 3

Ingredients:
- 1 tbsp finely ground graham cracker crumbs
- 2 tsp pureed bread and dessert mix
- ⅛ tsp sugar
- 1 ½ tbsp water
- 1 tsp vegetable oil
- 1 oz cream cheese
- 1 ½ tsp lemon juice
- 1 tbsp + 1 tsp powdered sugar
- 3 tbsp curd or pie filling of lemon
- 1 drop vanilla extract
- 3 tbsp whipped cream
- 2 tsp milk

Instructions:
1. Use quite a bit of non-stick cooking spray to coat the pan.
2. Combine bread and dessert mix (texture-modified), sugar, as well as graham cracker crumbs. When the mixture looks like wet sand, put oil, then stir.
3. Stir quickly until the mixture starts to thicken while adding boiling water to the bread mixture.
4. For at least 15 minutes, cover and let the food chill at room temperature or inside the refrigerator.
5. Fill the pan with the cooled crust mix.
6. Push the crust onto the pan's sides after pressing it flat.
7. Place the crust in the freezer or fridge to harden up.
8. In a bowl used for mixing, combine the powdered sugar, cream cheese,

vanilla, and lemon juice. Beat till smooth. Scrape the spatula's sides clean.
9. After adding the milk, stir the mixture until smooth. After whipping the cream, fold it in.
10. For garnish, set aside a little portion of the filling.
11. Spread the remaining filling equally over the graham cracker crust. Frozen to a solid state.
12. Over the frozen filling, spread the lemon curd or lemon pie filling. Use more whipped cream or the remaining cream cheese mixture to garnish as needed.
13. Dessert should be cut and divided while still cold. Before serving, thoroughly thaw the servings.

Nutrients:
- **Calories:** 330 kcal
- **Total Fats:** 19 g
- **Saturated Fats:** 9 g
- **Cholesterol:** 40 mg
- **Sodium:** 200 mg
- **Carbs:** 37 g
- **Fibers:** 1 g
- **Sugar:** 24 g
- **Proteins:** 3 g

16. Meat Loaf Puree

Prep Time: 5 minutes
Cook Time: 0 minutes
Total Time: 5 minutes
Serving: 1
Level: 1

Ingredients:
- 1 boiled potato
- 3 oz meatloaf
- 1 cube beef bouillon
- 2 tbsp brown gravy
- 1 boiled carrot

Instructions:
1. Cube the meatloaf, potatoes, and carrots.
2. In a food processor, combine all the ingredients.
3. Mix until uniform.

Nutrients:
- **Calories:** 184 kcal
- **Total Fats:** 13 g
- **Saturated Fats:** 2 g
- **Cholesterol:** 25 mg
- **Sodium:** 843 mg
- **Carbs:** 7 g
- **Fibers:** 4 g
- **Sugar:** 1 g
- **Proteins:** 10 g

17. Chicken Tikka Masala with Sticky Rice

Prep Time: 50 minutes
Cook Time: 45 minutes
Total Time: 95 minutes
Serving: 5
Level: 3

Ingredients:

- 2 tsp gram masala
- 28 oz skinless, boneless chicken breasts
- 1 tbsp fresh ginger
- ½ tsp ground red chili powder
- 1 tsp ground cumin
- 1 tsp ground turmeric
- 1 cup plain yogurt
- 1 tsp salt
- 2 tbsp butter
- 2 tbsp canola oil or vegetable
- 1 large onion
- 1 tsp ground coriander
- 1 ½ tbsp finely grated garlic
- 1 ½ tsp gram masala
- 1 cup sticky rice
- 14 oz tomato purée
- 1 ¼ cup heavy cream
- Water, as needed
- 1 tsp brown sugar
- Coriander or cilantro for garnish

Instructions:

1. Pour the necessary quantity of rice into a big bowl to make sticky rice. Add water till it is at room temperature and 3 inches over rice grains. Spend 6–24 hours soaking.
2. In a dish, combine the marinade ingredients. Add the chicken, then let it sit in the marinade for 10 minutes to 1 hour.
3. Sticky rice should be drained of its water. Put parchment paper into a steamer basket. Over a big saucepan of water that is boiling, place the basket. Steam under a cover for approximately 30–45 minutes. Before serving, keep it covered.
4. In a big non-stick skillet, heat the oil on medium to high heat. Add the chicken in batches and cook for 3 minutes on each side or until browned. Place aside.
5. Melt butter inside a pan over a high temperature. Once translucent and tender, cook onions.

Nutrients:

- **Calories:** 450 kcal
- **Total Fats:** 7.8 g
- **Saturated Fats:** 2.6 g
- **Cholesterol:** 22 mg
- **Sodium:** 1 g
- **Carbs:** 57 g
- **Fibers:** 7.6 g
- **Sugar:** 2 g
- **Proteins:** 31 g

18. Roasted Cauliflower Macaroni and Cheese

Prep Time: 20 minutes
Cook Time: 30–35 minutes
Total Time: 50–55 minutes
Serving: 4
Level: 3

Ingredients:

- 20 oz chopped cauliflower florets
- 12 oz macaroni pasta noodles
- 2 cups dairy milk, any percentage
- 2 tbsp flour
- ¾ cup chicken stock
- Salt and pepper to taste
- 1 cup Italian cheese blend
- 2 tbsp butter
- 3 tbsp olive oil
- 1 bunch white and green parts, separated and sliced green onions

Instructions:

1. Set the oven's temperature to 425°F. 2 baking sheets should be lined with aluminum foil and gently greased using olive oil.
2. On baking pans, distribute cauliflower florets, excluding any crumbly pieces. Add a good amount of pepper and salt and spray with olive oil. For 20 to twenty-five minutes, roast until extremely soft in the oven.
3. Bring water inside a big saucepan to a boil. Pasta noodles and a dash of salt should be added to the saucepan. Cook for a very long time while occasionally stirring. Pasta that has been drained should be added back to the pot.
4. In a big non-stick pan heated to a medium-high temperature, brown the onion whites after adding them. Add and melt the butter. Cook for 1 to 2 minutes while stirring in the flour. Pour the milk in gradually and whisk to mix. Stir in the chicken stock, then cook until thickened. Put the thickener if necessary.
5. Add cheese after removing from heat. To make it creamier, if necessary, add more milk, around 1/2 to 3/4 cup. Add pepper and salt to taste.
6. With some cauliflower set aside for the topping, combine the cheese mixture in the pan with the pasta. The mixture should be transferred to a baking dish suitable for the oven that has been buttered. On top, spread the leftover cauliflower. Bake for 5–7 minutes or until bubbling.
7. Serve alongside onion greens as a garnish.

Nutrients:

- **Calories:** 150 kcal
- **Total Fats:** 8 g
- **Saturated Fats:** 5 g
- **Cholesterol:** 44 mg
- **Sodium:** 290 mg
- **Carbs:** 12 g
- **Fibers:** 2 g
- **Sugar:** 3 g
- **Proteins:** 7 g

19. Black Bean Soup

Prep Time: 15 minutes
Cook Time: 25 minutes
Total Time: 40 minutes
Serving: 4
Level: 2

Ingredients:

- 1 large thinly sliced onion
- 3 tbsp olive oil
- 1 ½ tsp sea salt
- 12 sprigs fresh chopped coriander
- 3 garlic cloves, minced
- 1 tsp ground cumin
- ½ tsp chipotle chili powder
- ½ tsp chili powder ground
- 2 (14-oz) cans of black beans
- Avocado crème, as much as you want
- 3 cups chicken stock
- ¼ cup water
- Sour cream or Greek yogurt for topping
- ½ whole avocado
- ¼ tsp salt
- 2 limes

Instructions:

1. Over moderately high heat, warm the olive oil inside a large saucepan or casserole dish. Sauté for 5 minutes after adding the onion and salt. To avoid the onions from becoming too brown, toss them often.
2. Add the garlic, spices, and coriander. Check to make sure nothing is burning after 5 minutes of cooking with the cover on.
3. Put chicken stock and black beans. After bringing the soup to a boil, let it simmer for 15 minutes uncovered.
4. Mash the avocado and combine it with the juice of 2 limes, water, and salt to produce avocado crème.
5. Soup may be blended in a dish itself with a blender until it is completely lump-free and extremely smooth. If soup needs thickening, add food thickener. Put chicken stock, then blend if you want a thinner soup.
6. Put the soup in bowls, top with chosen garnishes and avocado crème, then serve.

Nutrients:

- **Calories:** 253 kcal
- **Total Fats:** 6.3 g
- **Saturated Fats:** 1.3 g
- **Cholesterol:** 2.5 mg
- **Sodium:** 765 mg
- **Carbs:** 36 g
- **Fibers:** 12 g
- **Sugar:** 2.2 g
- **Proteins:** 13 g

20. Italian Chicken Puree

Prep Time: 10 minutes
Cook Time: 30 secs
Total Time: 10 min 30 secs
Serving: 1
Level: 1

Ingredients:

- 3 tbsp tomato sauce
- Salt and pepper to taste
- ½ cup cooked chicken
- 1–1/2 tsp Italian seasoning

Instructions:

1. Blend or process all of the components in a blender or food processor. Alternatively, you might mash them manually with a fork.
2. Microwave the entire mixture for about 30 seconds after it is properly combined and soft.

Nutrients:

- **Calories:** 106 kcal
- **Total Fats:** 4 g
- **Saturated Fats:** 1 g
- **Cholesterol:** 26 mg
- **Sodium:** 656 mg
- **Carbs:** 3 g
- **Fibers:** 1 g
- **Sugar:** 1 g
- **Proteins:** 13 g

21. Black Bean and Red Pepper Puree

Prep Time: 10 minutes
Cook Time: 5 minutes
Total Time: 15 minutes
Serving: 1
Level: 1

Ingredients:

- 3 tbsp enchilada sauce
- 3 tbsp chicken broth
- 1 cup black beans
- 4 tbsp red pepper, roasted and chopped

Instructions:

1. On medium heat, combine the peppers, beans, and 1/2 enchilada sauce in a skillet.
2. Put chicken broth once the ingredients have finished cooking.
3. Mix the ingredients with a blender once the heat has been removed.
4. Before serving, place the puree into a serving dish and top with the remaining enchilada sauce.

Nutrients:

- **Calories:** 85 kcal
- **Total Fats:** 1.5 g
- **Saturated Fats:** 0.3 g

- » **Cholesterol:** 123 mg
- » **Sodium:** 528 mg
- » **Carbs:** 16 g
- » **Fibers:** 1 g
- » **Sugar:** 9 g
- » **Proteins:** 3 g

22. Pureed Salmon

Prep Time: 10 minutes
Cook Time: 15 minutes
Total Time: 25 minutes
Serving: 2
Level: 1

Ingredients:

- » ½ oz white wine dry
- » ½ cup water
- » ½ sliced lemon
- » 1 oz sliced onion
- » 1 oz cream
- » 2 springs parsley
- » 1 ½ tsp salt
- » 1 tsp of pepper
- » 3 oz salmon steaks
- » 2 springs dill
- » Pepper

Instructions:

1. Inside a saucepan, combine water, onion, wine, lemon, pepper, salt, parsley, and dill.
2. Once it begins to boil, turn down the heat, then cover the pan and cook for 10 minutes.
3. Salmon steaks should be added, covered, and simmered for 5 minutes.
4. Mix the ingredients inside a food blender after adding cream.

Nutrients:

- » **Calories:** 142 kcal
- » **Total Fats:** 6.3 g
- » **Saturated Fats:** 1.2 g
- » **Cholesterol:** 67 mg
- » **Sodium:** 346 mg
- » **Carbs:** 0 g
- » **Fibers:** 0 g
- » **Sugar:** 0 g
- » **Proteins:** 20 g

23. Sausage and Onions

Prep Time: 5 minutes
Cook Time: 10 minutes
Total Time: 15 minutes
Serving: 1
Level: 4

Ingredients:

- 2 oz onions
- 1 tsp chopped sage
- 3 oz skinned and uncooked sausage meat
- 1 tsp gravy browning
- ½ cup water

Instructions:

1. In a pan, combine the sausage, water, onions, and sage. Cook it for about 10 minutes.
2. Allow it to cool somewhat before adding gravy browning, then blend until smooth.
3. To acquire varied tastes, you might, if you'd like, add white sauce, tomato sauce, mustard, or gravy to the mixture.

Nutrients:

- **Calories:** 339 kcal
- **Total Fats:** 27 g
- **Saturated Fats:** 10 g
- **Cholesterol:** 84 mg
- **Sodium:** 746 mg
- **Carbs:** 5.8 g
- **Fibers:** 1 g
- **Sugar:** 3 g
- **Proteins:** 17 g

Chapter 4
Dinner Recipes

1. Easy-Peasy Chicken

Prep Time: 5 minutes
Cook Time: 0 minutes
Total Time: 5 minutes
Serving: 1
Level: 2

Ingredients:

- ½ cup canned vegetables
- ½ cup shredded cooked chicken
- ½ cup milk

Instructions:

1. Each of the components should be placed in a food processor or blender and well blended. Enjoy.

Nutrients:

- **Calories:** 860 kcal
- **Total Fats:** 38 g
- **Saturated Fats:** 20 g
- **Cholesterol:** 183 mg
- **Sodium:** 830 mg
- **Carbs:** 75 g
- **Fibers:** 6 g
- **Sugar:** 6 g
- **Proteins:** 54 g

2. Lobster Bisque

Prep Time: 5 minutes
Cook Time: 5 minutes
Total Time: 10 minutes
Serving: 2
Level: 1

Ingredients:

- 1 can lobster meat
- 2 ½ cups milk
- 1 tbsp flour
- A pinch pepper
- 1 tbsp butter
- ⅛ tsp celery salt
- 1 tsp salt
- ¼ tsp paprika

Instructions:

1. Use a food processor or blender to combine every ingredient other than the tinned lobster flesh.
2. Remix the mixture after adding the lobster flesh.
3. The next step is to place everything into a pot and heat it while stirring.
4. The soup has to be strained before it is suitable to consume.

Nutrients:

- **Calories:** 310 kcal
- **Total Fats:** 24 g
- **Saturated Fats:** 15 g
- **Cholesterol:** 115 mg
- **Sodium:** 680 mg

- » **Carbs:** 13 g
- » **Fibers:** 1 g
- » **Sugar:** 1 g
- » **Proteins:** 12 g

3. Beef and Sweet Potato Puree with Thyme

Prep Time: 40 minutes
Cook Time: 10 minutes
Total Time: 50 minutes
Serving: 2
Level: 2

Ingredients:
- » 2 cubed and peeled sweet potatoes
- » 8 oz beef steak, cubed
- » 1 tbsp thyme leaves
- » 2 cups beef stock reduced-sodium

Instructions:
1. The first step is to combine every 1 of the components in a medium pot.
2. Bring it to a boil on a medium heat setting on your stove.
3. After that, turn down the heat to a boil and let it sit for 25 to 35 minutes.
4. When the sweet potato and steak cubes are cooked, remove them from the fire.
5. Transfer the contents to a food processor or blender after allowing it to cool down for several minutes.
6. If additional meat stock is required, blend until totally smooth puree forms.

Nutrients:
- » **Calories:** 249 kcal
- » **Total Fats:** 1.5 g
- » **Saturated Fats:** 0.7g
- » **Cholesterol:** 0.5 mg
- » **Sodium:** 88 mg
- » **Carbs:** 58 g
- » **Fibers:** 8 g
- » **Sugar:** 18 g
- » **Proteins:** 9 g

4. Minced Meat Shepherd's Pie

Prep Time: 20 minutes
Cook Time: 30 minutes
Total Time: 50 minutes
Serving: 2
Level: 3

Ingredients:
- » 1 tsp onion powder
- » 12 oz bag ground beef minced
- » 1 tsp ground dry mustard
- » 1 tsp garlic, minced
- » ¼ tsp fine ground black pepper
- » ¼ tsp thyme leaves
- » ½ tsp salt
- » 2 tsp Worcestershire sauce
- » ¼ tsp oregano leaves
- » 1 ¾ cup tomato sauce
- » ¼ bag bulk pureed peas
- » ½ cup instant food thickener
- » 1 tbsp butter
- » 3 tbsp instant food thickener

- » ⅛ tsp salt
- » ¼ bag bulk pureed carrot
- » ⅛ tsp salt
- » 1 tbsp butter
- » Parsley finely chopped, for garnish
- » 2 cups potatoes, mashed
- » 3 tbsp instant food thickener
- » For garnish, red pepper or paprika

Instructions:

1. Spray cooking oil on the pan.
2. Combine onion powder, ground mustard, garlic powder, black pepper, thyme, salt, and oregano into ground minced beef that has been thawed.
3. Add tomato sauce and Worcestershire sauce and mix well.
4. Stir in the thickener powder.
5. Put the meat mixture into the pan evenly.
6. Melted butter, thawed and heated bulk pureed peas, and salt should be combined.
7. Stir in the thickener powder.
8. Spread the meat mixture in the pan equally.
9. Salt, melted butter, and hot, frozen bulk pureed carrots should be combined.
10. Stir in the thickener powder.
11. Over the pea mixture in the pan, distribute or portion equally.
12. If preferred, top over mashed potatoes and paprika.
13. When the temperature hits 165°F and a knife put in the middle of the pan comes up clean, cover the pan securely with foil. Bake at 350°F or cook in a steamer.
14. 5 minutes should pass before cutting and dividing.

Nutrients:

- » **Calories:** 370 kcal
- » **Total Fats:** 18 g
- » **Saturated Fats:** 8 g
- » **Cholesterol:** 75 mg
- » **Sodium:** 1020 mg
- » **Carbs:** 34 g
- » **Fibers:** 6 g
- » **Sugar:** 7 g
- » **Proteins:** 21 g

5. Soft Potatoes

Prep Time: 10 minutes
Cook Time: 45 minutes
Total Time: 55 minutes
Serving: 6
Level: 3

Ingredients:

- » 6 tbsp melted butter
- » 3 lb peeled Yukon Gold potatoes
- » 1 tsp thyme dried
- » 1 tsp salt
- » ½ tsp rosemary dried
- » 2 tbsp parsley chopped
- » 1 cup chicken broth
- » ½ tsp pepper
- » 2–3 garlic cloves

Instructions:

1. The oven should be heated to 475°F. Apply non-stick cooking oil to a sizable flat cookie pan.

2. Melted butter, rosemary, thyme, pepper, and salt should all be combined in a dish.
3. Cut potatoes into segments that are 3/4-1 inch in thickness, removing the edges. Stir together the butter and potatoes. Place on the baking tray that has been prepped in 1 layer.
4. For 15 minutes, roast the potatoes. Take potatoes out of the oven and turn them over. Once more, bake for 15 minutes in the oven.
5. Take the potatoes out of the oven and turn them once more. Return the skillet to the oven gingerly after adding the stock and garlic. Potatoes should be soft after an extra 10–15 minutes of roasting. Serve after adding parsley.

Nutrients:
- **Calories:** 22 kcal
- **Total Fats:** 0 g
- **Saturated Fats:** 0 g
- **Cholesterol:** 0 mg
- **Sodium:** 4 mg
- **Carbs:** 5 g
- **Fibers:** 1 g
- **Sugar:** 0 g
- **Proteins:** 1 g

6. Pureed Pasta with Chicken Alfredo

Prep Time: 10 minutes
Cook Time: 20 minutes
Total Time: 30 minutes
Serving: 1
Level: 2

Ingredients:
- ¼ cup alfredo sauce
- 1 tsp instant food thickener
- ½ cup ground chicken thawed
- ½ cup thickened bulk pureed pasta blend

Instructions:
1. Stir well to include ground chicken and creamy Alfredo sauce.
2. Heat thoroughly until the inside reaches 165°F.
3. Add roughly 1 teaspoon of instant food thickener, as required, and mix well.
4. Keep it at 135°F hot or more for service.
5. Prepare bulk thickened pureed pasta. Blend as directed, then set aside for use.
6. Add approximately ⅔ cup of the chicken and Alfredo sauce combination to the pasta.
7. If desired, add shredded Parmesan cheese as a garnish.

Nutrients:
- **Calories:** 390 kcal
- **Total Fats:** 26 g
- **Saturated Fats:** 9 g
- **Cholesterol:** 115 mg
- **Sodium:** 769 mg
- **Carbs:** 19 g
- **Fibers:** 0 g
- **Sugar:** 2 g
- **Proteins:** 18 g

7. Sweet and Sour Chicken

Prep Time: 15 minutes
Cook Time: 10 minutes
Total Time: 25 minutes
Serving: 1
Level: 2

Ingredients:

- 4 tbsp prepared sweet and sour sauce
- ½ cup thawed minced chicken
- Prepared sweet and sour sauce, as needed for garnish
- ½ of 2.5 oz frozen pureed-shaped pineapple
- ½ cup pureed rice

Instructions:

1. Combine sweet and sour sauce with thawed and minced chicken. Heating to 165°F.
2. To reach the correct consistency, you may, if necessary, add a tiny quantity of instant food and beverage thickener.
3. Make bite-sized chunks of pureed frozen-shaped pineapple.
4. Heat pureed rice to 165°F.
5. On a dish, spoon ½ cup of the pureed rice mix. Add ½ cup of the chicken mixture to the rice.
6. Over the rice, spread the chopped pineapple chunks.
7. Add more sweet and sour sauce as a garnish.

Nutrients:

- **Calories:** 470 kcal
- **Total Fats:** 15 g
- **Saturated Fats:** 3.5 g
- **Cholesterol:** 65 mg
- **Sodium:** 900 mg
- **Carbs:** 69 g
- **Fibers:** 1 g
- **Sugar:** 46 g
- **Proteins:** 16 g

8. Country BBQ Sundae

Prep Time: 20 minutes
Cook Time: 25 minutes
Total Time: 45 minutes
Serving: 6
Level: 4

Ingredients:

- ¼ cup heavy-duty mayonnaise
- 3 cups mashed potatoes prepared
- 2 tbsp yellow mustard
- 3 cups thawed minced pork
- 8 tbsp (1 stick) salted butter
- 2 tbsp sweet pickle brine
- ½ of 2lb bag thawed pureed corn
- 12 oz sweet BBQ sauce

Instructions:

For the whipped potato salad:
1. Mayo, mustard, and sweet pickle juice should all be combined. Mix thoroughly after adding to the cooked mashed potatoes.
2. Place in the fridge with a cover.

For BBQ pork:
1. Cook minced pork to 165°F.
2. In a big bowl, combine the heated pork with the BBQ sauce and mix to combine. Keep heated and set aside.

For corn:
1. Preheat the pureed corn to 165°F. Dispense into a container, then cover and reserve.
2. Melt the butter in a skillet over a medium-high flame while the corn is cooling.
3. During this procedure, it's crucial to keep an eye on the butter since it might burn easily.
4. When the butter starts to turn brown and emits a toasty, nutty scent, watch it carefully and take it away from the heat right away.
5. Corn should be combined well with browned butter after being added.

For assembly:
1. Select a bowl with a wall.
2. Pour 1/3 cup of corn puree into the basin.
3. Top with approximately half a cup of creamed potato salad and 12 cups of barbecued pork on top.
4. Try piping creamed potato salad into a swirling manner over the BBQ pork to improve the presentation.
5. Serve warm after reheating to serving temperature.

Nutrients:
- **Calories:** 640 kcal
- **Total Fats:** 37 g
- **Saturated Fats:** 17 g
- **Cholesterol:** 110 mg
- **Sodium:** 1300 mg
- **Carbs:** 62 g
- **Fibers:** 3 g
- **Sugar:** 5 g
- **Proteins:** 19 g

9. BBQ Pork

Prep Time: 10 minutes
Cook Time: 10 minutes
Total Time: 20 minutes
Serving: 3
Level: 4

Ingredients:
- 3.4 oz BBQ Sauce
- 0.32 lb Bulk Pureed Pork

Instructions:
1. Heat pureed pork to 165°F in the steamer.
2. Put the pureed pork in the steam pan after removing the bag.
3. Stir heated BBQ sauce into the pureed meat before serving.
4. When serving at 135°F or above, keep it warm.

Nutrients:
- **Calories:** 418 kcal
- **Total Fats:** 11 g
- **Saturated Fats:** 3 g
- **Cholesterol:** 87 mg
- **Sodium:** 1.7 g
- **Carbs:** 47 g
- **Fibers:** 3 g
- **Sugar:** 38 g
- **Proteins:** 33 g

10. Spiced Carrot and Lentil Soup

Prep Time: 10 minutes
Cook Time: 17 minutes
Total Time: 27 minutes
Serving: 4
Level: 3

Ingredients:
- A pinch chili flakes
- 2 tsp cumin seeds
- 1.23 lb carrots
- 2 tbsp olive oil
- 1 cup milk
- 4 cups vegetable stock
- 0.30 lb red lentils

Instructions:
1. 2 tablespoons of cumin seeds and a sprinkling of red chili peppers should be dry-fried for 1 minute until they begin to bounce around the skillet and unleash their fragrances.
2. With a spatula, remove about half and put it away. Shredded carrots, red lentils, veggie stock, and milk should all be added to the skillet and brought to a simmer.
3. To mellow and swell the legumes, cook for 15 minutes.
4. Use a stick mixer or a blender to puree the broth.
5. Finish with a spoonful of basic yogurt and a sprinkle of the saved roasted seasonings after seasoning to taste.

Nutrients:
- **Calories:** 238 kcal
- **Total Fats:** 7 g
- **Saturated Fats:** 1 g
- **Cholesterol:** 123 mg
- **Sodium:** 0 mg
- **Carbs:** 34 g
- **Fibers:** 5 g
- **Sugar:** 0 g
- **Proteins:** 11 g

11. Cullen Skink

Prep Time: 10 minutes
Cook Time: 35 minutes
Total Time: 45 minutes
Serving: 4
Level: 3

Ingredients:

- 1 onion
- 1 tbsp unsalted butter
- ½ bunch chives or parsley
- ½ lb smoked haddock
- 1 lb potatoes
- 1 cup whole milk
- 1 cup water

Instructions:

1. Over a moderate flame, melt butter. Add onion, then cook for 5 to 8 minutes or until transparent but not caramelized.
2. Bring to simmer potatoes and 1 cup of water. Simmer for 10 to 15 minutes on a low fire.
3. Place haddock in a different skillet and cover using milk in the meantime.
4. Cook for 5 minutes.
5. With a slanted utensil, remove the haddock from the milk, place it on a platter, and allow it to slightly chill.
6. Remove any bones and crumble into big chunks when it is cold enough to touch.
7. Cook for additional 5 minutes after adding the saved milk as well as haddock to the potato combination in the skillet.
8. To serve, season along with chives or parsley.

Nutrients:

- **Calories:** 206 kcal
- **Total Fats:** 6 g
- **Saturated Fats:** 4 g
- **Cholesterol:** 12 mg
- **Sodium:** 0 g
- **Carbs:** 21 g
- **Fibers:** 3 g
- **Sugar:** 6 g
- **Proteins:** 17 g

12. Pureed Green Bean Casserole

Prep Time: 10 minutes
Cook Time: 20–30 minutes
Total Time: 30–40 minutes
Serving: 6
Level: 4

Ingredients:

- ½–10.5 oz can mushroom soup cream
- ½ bag green beans pureed
- 1–2 tbsp water or milk
- ¼ tsp black pepper
- ¼ tsp salt
- 1 ½ cup French-fried onions

Instructions:

1. French-fried onions should be processed in a food processor to a smooth purée. Cut in half, then put aside.
2. Mix half of the onions, pepper, salt, and 1/2 of the cream of the mushroom soup with the pureed bulk green beans. To blend, thoroughly stir.
3. Spread the mixture into the cooking spray-coated pan.
4. Over the green beans, equally spread the remaining 1/2 of the cream of the mushroom soup.
5. To make the leftover fried onions smooth yet spreadable, add milk or water.
6. Onions may be spread, dolloped, or piped onto the dish.
7. Until the internal temperature is 165°F, bake covered at 350°F.

Nutrients:

- **Calories:** 180 kcal
- **Total Fats:** 8 g
- **Saturated Fats:** 4 g
- **Cholesterol:** 0 mg
- **Sodium:** 410 mg
- **Carbs:** 15 g
- **Fibers:** 1 g
- **Sugar:** 2 g
- **Proteins:** 1 g

13. Pureed Lasagna

Prep Time: 20 minutes
Cook Time: 40 minutes
Total Time: 60 minutes
Serving: 1
Level: 2

Ingredients:

- 1 ½ tsp butter
- 1/3 cup water
- 1 tbsp pasta mix pureed pasta
- 1 tbsp shredded mozzarella cheese
- 1 tbsp cottage cheese
- 1 tbsp food thickener
- 1 tsp grated Parmesan cheese

- » 1 tsp parmesan cheese grated for garnish
- » A dash salt
- » ⅛ tsp Italian seasoning
- » 2 oz ground seasoned beef
- » A dash pepper
- » 2 tsp food thickener
- » ⅔ cup seasoned tomato sauce or pasta sauce

Instructions:

1. Bring to a boil water and butter.
2. Add the bulk pureed pasta, then whisk to combine.
3. In a blender, blend mozzarella, cottage cheese, and Parmesan till completely smooth.
4. Add it to the pasta that has been made and combine by whisking.
5. Add the first quantity of thickener powder to the salt, Italian seasoning, and pepper.
6. Add to the cheese and pasta purée, then stir to blend completely.
7. Spread into the skillet or pan with frying spray. Place aside.
8. In a blender, blend tomato sauce and seasoned beef mince until completely smooth.
9. Add the remaining thickener powder, and blend just long enough to mix.
10. In the pan, spread equally over the pasta and cheese layer.
11. If preferred, top with more Parmesan cheese.
12. When the temperature hits 165°F, and a knife put in the middle of the pan comes up clean, cover the pan securely with foil. Bake to 350°F.
13. Before dividing into parts, let stand for 5 minutes.
14. If desired, add more warm sauce for pasta as a garnish.

Nutrients:

- » **Calories:** 420 kcal
- » **Total Fats:** 18 g
- » **Saturated Fats:** 8 g
- » **Cholesterol:** 70 mg
- » **Sodium:** 1160 mg
- » **Carbs:** 35 g
- » **Fibers:** 4 g
- » **Sugar:** 1 g
- » **Proteins:** 27 g

14. Hash of Turkey Sausage

Prep Time: 15 minutes
Cook Time: 25 minutes
Total Time: 40 minutes
Serving: 2
Level: 3

Ingredients:

- » 1 tsp minced dried onion
- » 6 oz sausage
- » 1 cup butternut squash
- » 1 cup broth (beef or chicken)
- » ¾ cup apple
- » Salt and pepper to taste
- » ¼ cup fresh minced spinach
- » ½ tsp instant food thickener

Instructions:

1. Spray cooking oil on the pan.
2. Cook till meat has browned and no more pink, then stir in sausage and chopped dry onion. Sausage should be broken up into extremely small pieces using a spatula.
3. Take the meat mixture out of the pan and save it.
4. Put broth into the heating pan, boil, and swirl to remove any bits of meat that may still be stuck to the bottom of the pan.
5. Boil after adding the chopped butternut squash. For 2 to 3 minutes, decrease the heat, then cover, and simmer.
6. Put the chopped apple, cover the pot, and cook for another 3 to 4 minutes, till the chunks of squash and apple are completely cooked and soft.
7. Stir in the spinach that has been finely chopped.
8. Use pepper and salt to taste.
9. Stir the ingredients in the pan after adding instant food thickener to help any leftover broth become thicker.
10. Hold it hot for serving at about 135°F.

Nutrients:

- **Calories:** 340 kcal
- **Total Fats:** 23 g
- **Saturated Fats:** 8 g
- **Cholesterol:** 60 mg
- **Sodium:** 740 mg
- **Carbs:** 19 g
- **Fibers:** 4 g
- **Sugar:** 8 g
- **Proteins:** 15 g

15. Pureed Cheesy Vegetable Dish

Prep Time: 10 minutes
Cook Time: 25 minutes
Total Time: 35 minutes
Serving: 1
Level: 2

Ingredients:

- 1 tsp vegetable oil
- 1 tbsp onion
- ¼ cup cauliflower
- 2 tbsp carrots
- ¼ cup broccoli
- ¼ tsp garlic, minced
- 1 tbsp cream cheese
- ¼ cup broth
- 1/3 cup shredded cheddar cheese
- 1 tsp food thickener instant
- 1 ½ tsp Parmesan cheese
- Paprika, for garnish
- A dash salt
- ½ tsp ground mustard
- A dash pepper

Instructions:

1. Make sure the minced broccoli, carrots, and cauliflower are cooked.
2. Onion and garlic are sautéed in hot oil until tender.
3. Fill the pan with broth and prepare minced veggies. For 2 to 3 minutes, boil.
4. Put cheddar cheese, cream cheese, and Parmesan cheese after lowering the heat. Cheeses should be well dissolved and combined while simmering and stirring.
5. When the mixture begins to thicken, put an instant thickener for food and stir.
6. Add the salt, pepper, and mustard powder.
7. Hold it hot for serving at 135°F.
8. One round scoop should be used per serving.
9. Add paprika to each plate as garnish.

Nutrients:

- **Calories:** 290 kcal
- **Total Fats:** 11 g
- **Saturated Fats:** 11 g
- **Cholesterol:** 55 mg
- **Sodium:** 830 mg
- **Carbs:** 8 g
- **Fibers:** 2 g
- **Sugar:** 2 g
- **Proteins:** 13 g

16. Creamy Fortified Butternut Squash Soup

Prep Time: 15 minutes
Cook Time: 20 minutes
Total Time: 35 minutes
Serving: 2
Level: 1

Ingredients:

- 2 tbsp food and beverage thickener
- 10 oz soup butternut squash
- 8 oz vanilla nutrition shakes

Instructions:

1. In a container, mix the soup and nutritional shake.
2. Stirring periodically, heat the mix on the stove or inside a microwave till it is hot.
3. Take the soup out from the stove and quickly whisk or mix in the instant food and beverage thickener until well combined.
4. To ensure that the soup keeps the proper degree of thickness, present at a temperature higher than 135°F.

Nutrients:

- **Calories:** 310 kcal
- **Total Fats:** 11 g
- **Saturated Fats:** 11 g
- **Cholesterol:** 5 mg
- **Sodium:** 470 mg
- **Carbs:** 44 g
- **Fibers:** 3 g
- **Sugar:** 12 g
- **Proteins:** 12 g

17. Turkey and Dumpling Soup

Prep Time: 10 minutes
Cook Time: 20 minutes
Total Time: 30 minutes
Serving: 2
Level: 1

Ingredients:

- 2 chopped celery ribs
- 1 tbsp olive oil
- 1 ½ lb red potatoes
- ½ cup onion chopped
- ½ tsp pepper
- 3 ½ cups mixed vegetables frozen
- 2 cartons chicken broth reduced-sodium
- ⅔ cup 2% milk
- ½ tsp dried thyme
- 2 cups baking/biscuit mix
- 2 ½ cups cooked chicken or turkey shredded

Instructions:

1. Oil should be heated to a moderate temperature in a 6-quart stockpot before celery and onion are added.
2. Boil while stirring in the potatoes, mixed veggies, spices, and broth. Lower heat; cook potatoes covered for 8 to 10 minutes till almost tender.
3. Add the turkey and boil the mixture.
4. Baking mix and milk should be stirred till the dough becomes soft.
5. Drop it by tablespoonful over boiling soup. Cook it covered on a low flame for 8 to 10 minutes.

Nutrients:

- **Calories:** 176 kcal
- **Total Fats:** 4 g
- **Saturated Fats:** 1.3 g
- **Cholesterol:** 88 mg
- **Sodium:** 527 mg
- **Carbs:** 17 g
- **Fibers:** 1 g
- **Sugar:** 1 g
- **Proteins:** 17 g

18. Macaroni and Cheese

Prep Time: 20 minutes
Cook Time: 25 minutes
Total Time: 45 minutes
Serving: 4
Level: 2

Ingredients:

- 5 tbsp butter
- 1 ½ cup elbow macaroni uncooked
- ½ tsp salt
- 3 tbsp flour all-purpose
- 2 tbsp bread crumbs dry
- 1 ½ cup whole milk

- » ¼ tsp pepper
- » 2 oz cubed cheese
- » 1 cup cheddar cheese shredded

Instructions:

1. Macaroni should be prepared as directed on the packaging.
2. In the meanwhile, melt 4 tablespoons of butter in a skillet over a moderate flame.
3. When smooth, stir in the salt, flour, and pepper. Add milk gradually.
4. Cook and stir for 2 minutes at a time till it's thickened, after bringing it to a boil.
5. Lower the heat. Add cheeses and stir until they are completely melted. Rinse the macaroni.
6. Put the macaroni inside a 1–1/2 qt. oven dish that has been buttered.
7. Add cheese sauce to pasta and combine thoroughly.
8. Add the breadcrumbs after melting the remaining butter. Add some on top.
9. Bake for 30 minutes at 375°F, uncovered, until cooked, and the crust is golden.

Nutrients:

- » **Calories:** 510 kcal
- » **Total Fats:** 29 g
- » **Saturated Fats:** 16 g
- » **Cholesterol:** 96 mg
- » **Sodium:** 590 mg
- » **Carbs:** 39 g
- » **Fibers:** 2 g
- » **Sugar:** 4 g
- » **Proteins:** 24 g

19. Cold-Day Chicken Noodle Soup

Prep Time: 10 minutes
Cook Time: 15 minutes
Total Time: 25 minutes
Serving: 2
Level: 2

Ingredients:

- » 2 chopped celery ribs
- » 1 tbsp canola oil
- » 1 medium chopped onion,
- » 2 medium chopped carrots
- » 1 tbsp parsley minced
- » ½ tsp dried basil
- » 8 cups chicken broth reduced-sodium
- » 3 cups uncooked egg noodles (whole-wheat)
- » ¼ tsp pepper
- » 3 cups rotisserie chicken coarsely chopped

Instructions:

1. Oil should be heated over medium-high heat inside a 6-qt stockpot.
2. Add carrots, celery, and onion; stir-fry for 5 to 7 minutes, till the vegetables are soft.
3. Boil the basil, pepper, and broth. Noodles are added and cooked for 12 to 14 minutes.
4. Chicken and parsley are added; heat well.

Nutrients:
- **Calories:** 195 kcal
- **Total Fats:** 6 g
- **Saturated Fats:** 1 g
- **Cholesterol:** 47 mg
- **Sodium:** 639 mg
- **Carbs:** 16 g
- **Fibers:** 3 g
- **Sugar:** 2 g
- **Proteins:** 21 g

20. POTATOES WITH CHEDDAR

Prep Time: 10 minutes
Cook Time: 20 minutes
Total Time: 3 minutes
Serving: 2
Level: 3

Ingredients:
- 1 ¼ cup half-and-half cream
- 3 lb potatoes
- 3 cups cheddar cheese extra-sharp and shredded
- 1 tsp salt
- 3 tbsp butter
- Water, as needed

Instructions:
1. Inside a 6-qt. stockpot, add the potatoes and enough water to fully cover them up to a boil.
2. Lower heat; cook for 15 to 20 minutes, uncovered.
3. Butter, cream, and salt should be heated in a pot while stirring periodically until the butter has melted.
4. Return the potatoes to the saucepan after draining. Add the cream mixture gradually while you mash your potatoes. Add cheese and stir.

Nutrients:
- **Calories:** 523 kcal
- **Total Fats:** 33 g
- **Saturated Fats:** 17 g
- **Cholesterol:** 86 mg
- **Sodium:** 1247 mg
- **Carbs:** 42 g
- **Fibers:** 3 g
- **Sugar:** 4 g
- **Proteins:** 15 g

21. Grilled Cheese and Pickle Sandwich

Prep Time: 25 minutes
Cook Time: 30 minutes
Total Time: 55 minutes
Serving: 4
Level: 4

Ingredients:

- 1 lb whole milk
- 0.22 lb white bread
- 1.10 lb onions
- 0.11 lb sandwich pickle
- 0.11 lb oil
- 1/5 tsp carrageenan iota
- 0.66 lb double cream
- 0.66 lb strong cheddar cheese
- 0.22 lb full-fat milk

Instructions:

1. For making the puree of pickled onions and toast, make toast purée first: The bread should be finely ground before baking at 200°C in a heated oven till it becomes a deep golden-brown color.
2. Put toasted crumbs into the mixer, add milk, and pulse-process until the ingredients are well combined and the consistency is smooth.
3. Place the bowl containing the toast puree top with cling film. Make sure cling film contacts the outside to avoid the formation of the skin.
4. For making the puree for onion pickle, in an oil-filled frying pan with a heavy bottom and medium-high heat, slice onions and caramelize them. It could take 10 to 15 minutes.
5. The pickle and onions should be blended in a fine-mesh setting until entirely smooth till the onions are a deep golden-brown color.
6. To complete the bread on onion pickled puree that's no stickier, combine the purees of the pickles and toast.
7. Shred cheddar and put it out evenly onto a silicon surface to make of puree of grilled cheese.
8. Cook in a hot pan until bubbling and golden brown. Take out and let cool.
9. Split up the cooked cheese that has now cooled and whisk it into cream and milk in a large pan. Heat to boil while stirring occasionally.
10. As soon as the mixture begins to boil, turn off the heat, then let it sit for a while so the flavor of the grilled cheese may meld.
11. After cooling, pass the mixture through a small sieve to get rid of any cheese chunks.
12. Put it back to boil in a skillet, then add more seasoning and Carrageenan Iota.
13. After boiling, transfer the mixture to a basin and let it cool.

Nutrients:

- **Calories:** 137 kcal
- **Total Fats:** 14 g
- **Saturated Fats:** 3 g
- **Cholesterol:** 88 mg
- **Sodium:** 1849 mg
- **Carbs:** 61 g
- **Fibers:** 2 g
- **Sugar:** 18 g
- **Proteins:** 8 g

22. Braised Carrots

Prep Time: 5 minutes
Cook Time: 5 minutes
Total Time: 10 minutes
Serving: 1
Level: 1

Ingredients:

- Food thickener
- 4 cups vegetable/beef/lamb/chicken stock
- 1.10 lb carrots

Instructions:

1. Remove the carrot's stalk tip, peel it, and slice it into 5mm-thick pieces.
2. Tenderize the carrot by cooking it for a long time in the right stock.
3. Mix cooked carrots on a fine-mesh setting in an immersion blender until totally smooth. Add thickener if thick consistency is needed. Strain and set aside the stock.

Nutrients:

- **Calories:** 156 kcal
- **Total Fats:** 7 g
- **Saturated Fats:** 5 g
- **Cholesterol:** 19 mg
- **Sodium:** 252 mg
- **Carbs:** 22 g
- **Fibers:** 4 g
- **Sugar:** 15 g
- **Proteins:** 1.4 g

23. Lyonnaise Potatoes

Prep Time: 10 minutes
Cook Time: 10 minutes
Total Time: 20 minutes
Serving: 2
Level: 3

Ingredients:

- 1 cup whole milk
- 2.2 lb potatoes
- 2 tbsp oil
- Light lamb stock, as required
- 0.88 lb onions
- Salt, as required
- 3 garlic cloves
- 1 rosemary sprig
- Milk, as required

Instructions:

1. Potatoes should be peeled to remove the skins, then cut into 1 cm slices, then simmered until cooked in the seasoned water.
2. When potatoes are fully cooked, drain them and immediately put them into a strainer to process finely and remove any lumps.
3. Stir in the milk and sufficient lamb stock. Cover up to stay warm.
4. Cut the onions into tiny slices after removing the peel.
5. In a heavy-bottomed pan, combine the rosemary, onions, and a little salt. On medium heat, caramelize the

ingredients in oil; this might take up to 15 minutes.
6. Remove the garlic peel and mash it into a pulp before adding it to the onion mixture and cooking for an additional 5 minutes.
7. Remove rosemary stems after the garlic and onion mixture is fully cooked, then pulse the mixture in a blender until it is entirely smooth.
8. Combine an equal amount of potato puree plus half onion puree.
9. Potato and onion purees should be tasted and seasoned as needed.

Nutrients:
- **Calories:** 81 kcal
- **Total Fats:** 8 g
- **Saturated Fats:** 2.5 g
- **Cholesterol:** 5 mg
- **Sodium:** 300 mg
- **Carbs:** 27 g
- **Fibers:** 2 g
- **Sugar:** 5 g
- **Proteins:** 6 g

24. Turkey Burgers with Roasted Sweet Potatoes

Prep Time: 20 minutes
Cook Time: 20 minutes
Total Time: 40 minutes
Serving: 4
Level: 4

Ingredients:
- 2 tbsp olive oil
- 4 medium sweet potatoes
- Cayenne pepper, to taste
- 1 handful baby greens
- Salt and pepper, to taste
- ½ tsp Asian chili sauce
- 20 oz ground turkey
- 4 tsp fresh ginger
- 4 garlic cloves, minced
- ¼ cup finely chopped cilantro
- 4 tsp soy sauce
- 2 tsp Asian chili sauce for sauce
- 4 tbsp mayonnaise
- 4 buns

Instructions:
1. The oven should be heated to 450°F. Aluminum foil should be used to line the baking sheet. Lightly oil it with olive oil.
2. Sweet potatoes should be cut into 1\2-inch discs. Mix with some pepper, salt, and olive oil. Roast for approximately 25 minutes, rotating halfway through, till very tender. Remove from oven, then let it cool, but leave it on.
3. Ground turkey, ½ teaspoon of Asian chili sauce, garlic, cilantro, soy sauce, and ginger should all be combined in a dish. Add pepper and salt to taste. Make 4 patties out of the mixture.
4. In a big oven-safe pan, heat a small amount of olive oil on high heat. Add the patties and heat for 2–3 minutes each side or until browned. Burgers

should be baked for 5–7 minutes after being transferred to the oven.
5. Mayonnaise and Asian chili sauce are combined to make the sauce.
6. Take the hamburgers out of the oven. Put a meat thermometer in the burger to check for doneness. The recommended temperature is 165°F.
7. Put on buns over baby greens and baked sweet potatoes over the side. Pour sauce over hamburgers or use it as a dip.

Nutrients:
- **Calories:** 464 kcal
- **Total Fats:** 21 g
- **Saturated Fats:** 18 g
- **Cholesterol:** 678 mg
- **Sodium:** 12 mg
- **Carbs:** 30 g
- **Fibers:** 1 g
- **Sugar:** 2 g
- **Proteins:** 36 g

25. Chicken Croquettes with Mashed Potatoes

Prep Time: 30 minutes
Cook Time: 30 minutes
Total Time: 60 minutes
Serving: 6
Level: 4

Ingredients:
- 3 tbsp self-rising flour
- 2 tbsp butter
- 1 cup chicken broth
- 1 rib finely chopped celery
- 2 cups chopped and cooked chicken breasts
- 10 slices crusts removed white bread,
- Salt and pepper, to taste
- 2 eggs
- A dash peanut oil
- 4 tbsp butter
- A dash parsley, chopped
- 16 oz finely chopped mushrooms
- ½ to 1 cup cooking sherry
- 1 can mushroom soup cream
- 1 tbsp lemon juice
- A pinch kosher salt
- Black pepper freshly ground, as needed
- 4 large russet potatoes
- ½ cup dairy milk
- 4 tbsp butter,
- ½ cup full-fat sour cream

Instructions:
1. Remove the bread's crust. Cut the material into squares no bigger than 4 mm.
2. In a saucepan over low flame, mix 2 tablespoons of butter, chicken broth, and self-rising flour. Stir constantly until thick. When a sauce has to be thickened, add flour.
3. To the mixture, put cooked chicken, salt, celery, and pepper. For 2 hours, cover and chill.
4. Put the potatoes in a big saucepan and add water to cover them. Put a dash of salt Cook for 16–18 minutes, till it's very tender. Boil. Drain the water.

5. In a little saucepan on low flame, melt 4 tablespoons of butter. Add milk and mix. Pour over the potatoes, then stir to incorporate. Then stir in the sour cream. Place potatoes in a big basin. Use a handheld blender to whip the ingredients until they are creamy and lump-free. To taste, add pepper and salt to the food.
6. Take the chilled chicken mixture out of the fridge and then form it into croquettes. Croquettes are rolled in bread cubes after being dipped in beaten eggs. Put on your tray a wax paper covering. Before you're ready to cook, refrigerate.
7. Croquettes should be pan-fried with peanut oil till golden brown and uniformly cooked before serving. Once a crusty outer layer forms, turn the heat off. Before plating, remove excess oil by blotting it with paper towels.
8. In a pan, melt the last 4 tablespoons of butter. Add the mushrooms and cook them until tender. Once heated through, stir in the cream of mushroom soup, lemon juice, and half a cup of sherry. If required, add extra sherry to thin.
9. Add sauce to croquettes and parsley for decoration. Add mashed potatoes if desired.

Nutrients:
- **Calories:** 195 kcal
- **Total Fats:** 8.8 g
- **Saturated Fats:** 4.1 g
- **Cholesterol:** 113 mg
- **Sodium:** 194 mg
- **Carbs:** 3.3 g
- **Fibers:** 0.2 g
- **Sugar:** 0.4 g
- **Proteins:** 24.4 g

26. Pumpkin Crisp

Prep Time: 15 minutes
Cook Time: 60 minutes
Total Time: 75 minutes
Serving: 9
Level: 4

Ingredients:
- 1 cup evaporated milk
- 1 15-ounce can pumpkin
- ½ cup granulated sugar
- ½ tsp cinnamon
- 1 tsp vanilla
- Grated nutmeg, and whipped cream for topping

- » 1 cup butter
- » 1 box yellow cake mix with butter

Instructions:

1. Turn the oven on to 350°F.
2. Pumpkin, sugar, evaporated milk, vanilla, and cinnamon should all be mixed in a bowl. Fill an 11x7-inch baking dish.
3. Add the yellow cake mix equally. Add butter in a thin layer.
4. One hour of baking. Take it out from the oven, then wait 10 minutes for it to cool. To serve, top extra whipped cream and nutmeg, if desired.

Nutrients:

- » **Calories:** 270 kcal
- » **Total Fats:** 5 g
- » **Saturated Fats:** 3 g
- » **Cholesterol:** 45 mg
- » **Sodium:** 250 mg
- » **Carbs:** 51 g
- » **Fibers:** 2 g
- » **Sugar:** 42 g
- » **Proteins:** 5 g

27. Tangy Chicken Salad

Prep Time: 5 minutes
Cook Time: 0 minutes
Total Time: 5 minutes
Serving: 1
Level: 1

Ingredients:

- » 1 cup canned or cooked chicken
- » 2 tbsp Greek yogurt
- » 2 tbsp reduced-fat mayonnaise
- » ½ tsp onion powder
- » Salt and pepper, to taste

Instructions:

1. In a blender, puree the chicken till it becomes smooth.
2. To make it smooth, include yogurt, salt, pepper, mayonnaise, and onion powder.
3. If desired, add chives as a garnish.

Nutrients:

- » **Calories:** 380 kcal
- » **Total Fats:** 20 g
- » **Saturated Fats:** 3 g
- » **Cholesterol:** 70 mg
- » **Sodium:** 820 mg
- » **Carbs:** 27 g
- » **Fibers:** 4 g
- » **Sugar:** 11 g
- » **Proteins:** 22 g

28. Basic Fish Puree

Prep Time: 5 minutes
Cook Time: 0 minutes
Total Time: 5 minutes
Serving: 1
Level: 1

Ingredients:

- 1 tbsp mayonnaise reduced-fat
- Salt and pepper, to taste
- 1 cup canned or cooked fish, salmon or tuna
- 1 tbsp chopped green onions

Instructions:

1. Fish that has been canned or cooked should be processed in a blender till it becomes smooth.
2. Add the salt, mayonnaise, and pepper to the bowl with the ingredients.
3. Add some finely sliced green onions as a garnish.

Nutrients:

- **Calories:** 62 kcal
- **Total Fats:** 0.8 g
- **Saturated Fats:** 0 g
- **Cholesterol:** 5 mg
- **Sodium:** 63 mg
- **Carbs:** 10g
- **Fibers:** 1.7 g
- **Sugar:** 0.4 g
- **Proteins:** 4 g

29. Pureed Beef Stew

Prep Time: 10 minutes
Cook Time: 20 minutes
Total Time: 30 minutes
Serving: 1
Level: 1

Ingredients:

- 1 bag carrots or/and peas, frozen
- Salt and pepper, to taste
- 4 oz diced beef
- ½ cup beef gravy or broth

Instructions:

1. Cook 4 ounces of meat until tender.
2. Favorite veggies like carrots and peas may be boiled until they are soft.
3. Put ½ cup of gravy or beef broth.
4. Add salt and pepper and mix everything until the required consistency is reached.

Nutrients:
- **Calories:** 80 kcal
- **Total Fats:** 2 g
- **Saturated Fats:** 1 g
- **Cholesterol:** 15 mg
- **Sodium:** 390 mg
- **Carbs:** 5 g
- **Fibers:** 0 g
- **Sugar:** 1 g
- **Proteins:** 9 g

30. Tuna and Beans Puree

Prep Time: 5 minutes
Cook Time: 0 minutes
Total Time: 5 minutes
Serving: 1
Level: 2

Ingredients:
- 1 tin tuna
- 15 oz beans, cooked or canned
- Salt, to taste
- A pinch basil
- ½ lemon juice

Nutrients:
- **Calories:** 158 kcal
- **Total Fats:** 1.8 g
- **Saturated Fats:** 0.1 g
- **Cholesterol:** 26 mg
- **Sodium:** 478 mg
- **Carbs:** 20 g
- **Fibers:** 6 g
- **Sugar:** 1.3 g
- **Proteins:** 18.3 g

Instructions:
1. Blend all the components in a blender until they are well combined.
2. Add additional water if purée is excessively thick.

31. Chicken and Sweet Potato Puree

Prep Time: 15 minutes
Cook Time: 20 minutes
Total Time: 35 minutes
Serving: 2
Level: 2

Ingredients:

- 12 oz sweet potato
- Salt and other spices to taste
- 6 oz chicken breast
- Water, as required

Instructions:

1. In a saucepan filled with water that is boiling, cook your chicken for approximately 15 minutes till the flesh is fully cooked. Take it out of the water and allow it to cool.
2. Boiling water is used for cooking sweet potato inside a saucepan till it is extremely tender. Potatoes should be drained, but save the liquid.
3. In a blender, combine the potatoes, chicken, spices, and a little cooking liquid. Blend until smooth. If it's too thick, add additional water.

Nutrients:

- **Calories:** 90 kcal
- **Total Fats:** 1 g
- **Saturated Fats:** 0 g
- **Cholesterol:** 0 mg
- **Sodium:** 17 mg
- **Carbs:** 18 g
- **Fibers:** 1 g
- **Sugar:** 9 g
- **Proteins:** 2 g

Chapter 5
Snacks and Desert Recipes

1. Savory Beet Puree

Prep Time: 10 minutes
Cook Time: 40 minutes
Total Time: 50 minutes
Serving: 2
Level: 1

Ingredients:

- 1 cup Greek yogurt
- 1 beet
- 1 tsp dried fresh dill
- 1 tbsp olive oil
- Vegetable broth, as required
- A pinch salt
- ½ tsp garlic powder

Instructions:

1. Set your oven's temperature to 400°F.
2. Your beet should be cut, then tossed with a little salt and olive oil on a baking pan.
3. Bake the sheet of parchment paper in preheated oven until 40 minutes, flipping beet pieces with a spatula during the process.
4. Allow the beet slices to cool when you take them out of the oven.
5. Greek yogurt, garlic powder, and dill should then be added to them before placing them in the food processor.
6. Test to see whether the surface is sufficiently thin by giving it several pulses.
7. Feel free to add additional vegetable broth if it is too thick.

Nutrients:

- **Calories:** 151 kcal
- **Total Fats:** 10 g
- **Saturated Fats:** 3 g
- **Cholesterol:** 10.4 mg
- **Sodium:** 140 mg
- **Carbs:** 13.7 g
- **Fibers:** 2.53 g
- **Sugar:** 8.34 g
- **Proteins:** 2.6 g

2. Sweet Apple Bread Puree

Prep Time: 10 minutes
Cook Time: 0 minutes
Total Time: 10 minutes
Serving: 1
Level: 1

Ingredients:

- ½ tbsp flour for thickening
- ¾ cup apple juice
- 5 slices bread whole wheat

Instructions:

1. Put your bread pieces in the mixer or processor.
2. Pulse the bread and add the apple juice slowly.
3. After you've added every drop of juice, continue blending the mixture till it's smooth.
4. Add more flour or a thickening agent when the resulting mixture seems too thin.

Nutrients:

- **Calories:** 45 kcal
- **Total Fats:** 0.12 g
- **Saturated Fats:** 0 g
- **Cholesterol:** 0 mg
- **Sodium:** 0.67 mg
- **Carbs:** 10.67 g
- **Fibers:** 1 g
- **Sugar:** 8.58 g
- **Proteins:** 0.10 g

3. Decadent Dessert

Prep Time: 10 minutes
Cook Time: 0 minutes
Total Time: 10 minutes
Serving: 1
Level: 1

Ingredients:

- ½ cup cocoa powder
- 2 peeled ripe avocados
- A dash ground cinnamon
- ½ cup brown sugar
- ½ cup coconut milk
- 2 tsp vanilla extract

Instructions:

1. In a food processor or blender, mix all ingredients. Process till the mixture is smooth.
2. The pudding should then be placed in a jar and chilled for about 30 minutes in the refrigerator.

Nutrients:

- **Calories:** 290 kcal
- **Total Fats:** 13 g
- **Saturated Fats:** 7 g
- **Cholesterol:** 75 mg
- **Sodium:** 33 mg
- **Carbs:** 42 g
- **Fibers:** 0 g
- **Sugar:** 33 g
- **Proteins:** 5 g

4. Watermelon Sorbet

Prep Time: 5 minutes
Cook Time: 0 minutes
Total Time: 5 minutes
Serving: 1
Level: 1

Ingredients:

- 1 tsp agave or honey
- 2 tsp lime juice
- 1 cup chopped seedless watermelon

Instructions:

1. Spend at least a few hours or overnight freezing the diced watermelon.
2. When it's done, combine it alongside the lime juice, and honey in your food processor.
3. The sorbet should be processed until it is totally smooth.

Nutrients:

- **Calories:** 234 kcal
- **Total Fats:** 0.1 g
- **Saturated Fats:** 0 g
- **Cholesterol:** 0 mg
- **Sodium:** 20 mg
- **Carbs:** 61 g
- **Fibers:** 0.7 g
- **Sugar:** 58 g
- **Proteins:** 0.3 g

5. Minted Melon Smoothie

Prep Time: 5 minutes
Cook Time: 0 minutes
Total Time: 5 minutes
Serving: 1
Level: 1

Ingredients:

- ½ cup apple juice diluted
- 1 ½ cup honeydew melon
- 2 ½–3 cups ice
- Some sprigs fresh mint
- Honey or sugar, to taste

Instructions:

1. Apple juice, sugar, honeydew melon, ice, and mint should all be well blended.

Nutrients:

- **Calories:** 265 kcal
- **Total Fats:** 5.3 g
- **Saturated Fats:** 1 g
- **Cholesterol:** 4.8 mg
- **Sodium:** 131 mg
- **Carbs:** 48 g
- **Fibers:** 2.8 g
- **Sugar:** 21 g
- **Proteins:** 4.2 g

6. Vanilla Cake

Prep Time: 10 minutes
Cook Time: 30 minutes
Total Time: 40 minutes
Serving: 1
Level: 4

Ingredients:

- ½ tbsp vegetable oil
- 2 tbsp bread and dessert mix texture-modified
- ⅛ tsp vanilla extract
- 2 tbsp whipped topping
- ½ tsp sugar
- 3 tbsp milk
- 1/16 tsp almond extract

Instructions:

1. Spray the pan lightly using the non-stick spray for cooking.
2. Modified bread and dessert and sugar should be combined. In the mixing basin, combine. Stir in oil, almond extract, and vanilla until the mixture has the consistency of wet sand.
3. Put hot milk, then combine quickly while stirring.
4. Spread evenly after measuring out onto a skillet or muffin tin.
5. For at least 30 minutes, cover and leave the dish at room temperature or in the refrigerator.
6. Add whipped topping and slice into separate servings.

Nutrients:

- **Calories:** 150 kcal
- **Total Fats:** 8 g
- **Saturated Fats:** 1.5 g
- **Cholesterol:** 5 mg
- **Sodium:** 90 mg
- **Carbs:** 17 g
- **Fibers:** 0 g
- **Sugar:** 2 g
- **Proteins:** 4 g

7. Chocolate Cake

Prep Time: 10 minutes
Cook Time: 30 minutes
Total Time: 40 minutes
Serving: 1
Level: 3

Ingredients:

- ½ tbsp vegetable oil
- 2 tbsp bread and dessert mix texture-modified
- 1 tsp cocoa powder
- 2 tbsp whipped topping
- 3 tbsp milk
- ¾ tsp sugar
- 2 tsp chocolate syrup

Instructions:

1. Spray the pan lightly using a non-stick spray for cooking.
2. Sugar, bread, and dessert mix (Texture-Modified), and cocoa powder should all be combined in a mixing basin.
3. When the mixture looks like wet sand, put oil, then stir.
4. Pour heated milk over chocolate syrup, then whisk to combine.
5. The mixture will start to thicken once you quickly whisk in the milk.
6. Spread evenly after measuring out onto a skillet or muffin tin.
7. For at least 30 minutes, cover and leave the dish at room temperature or in the refrigerator.
8. Add whipped topping and slice into separate servings.

Nutrients:

- **Calories:** 190 kcal
- **Total Fats:** 8 g
- **Saturated Fats:** 1.5 g
- **Cholesterol:** 5 mg
- **Sodium:** 95 mg
- **Carbs:** 27 g
- **Fibers:** 1 g
- **Sugar:** 15 g
- **Proteins:** 4 g

8. Thickened Mocha Latte

Prep Time: 9 minutes
Cook Time: 1 minute
Total Time: 10 minutes
Serving: 1
Level: 2

Ingredients:

- 2 tsp cocoa powder
- 2 tsp sugar

- » Chocolate syrup and whipped topping, as needed for garnish
- » 6 oz hot water
- » 1 stick pack decaffeinated thickened coffee powder
- » ½ cup thickened dairy drink

Instructions:

1. Fill a cup with the decaffeinated (thickened) coffee powder.
2. Add 2 teaspoons of sugar plus 2 teaspoons of cocoa powder into the cup.
3. Stir vigorously till the powder is fully dissolved and drinks begin to thicken after adding 3/4 cup of boiling water.
4. Warm up dairy drink (thickened). Stir carefully after adding 1/2 cup of hot dairy drink to make the coffee thick.
5. If preferred, add some whipped cream and chocolate syrup to each dish.

Nutrients:

- » **Calories:** 140 kcal
- » **Total Fats:** 3 g
- » **Saturated Fats:** 2 g
- » **Cholesterol:** 10 mg
- » **Sodium:** 190 mg
- » **Carbs:** 25 g
- » **Fibers:** 1 g
- » **Sugar:** 16 g
- » **Proteins:** 5 g

9. Thickened Pumpkin Spice Latte

Prep Time: 10 minutes
Cook Time: 5 minutes
Total Time: 15 minutes
Serving: 1
Level: 1

Ingredients:

- » 3 tbsp pumpkin puree, canned
- » ½ cup thickened dairy drink
- » ¼ tsp blend pumpkin pie spice
- » 2 tsp sugar
- » ⅛ tsp vanilla extract
- » For garnish, nutmeg, pumpkin pie spice, or cinnamon
- » ½ cup coffee powder thickened
- » ¼ tsp extra nutmeg
- » 2 tbsp whipped topping

Instructions:

1. Pumpkin, pumpkin pie spice, vanilla, sugar, and dairy drink (thickened) are all mixed. Be cautious not to let the pot boil over while it is heated nearly to boiling.
2. Put ½ cup of thickened coffee that has been made in a mug.
3. Stir well after adding approximately two-thirds of a cup of the hot milk and pumpkin mixture to the mug of thickened coffee.
4. Add a whipped topping for garnish and a dash of your preferred spice.

Nutrients:

- » **Calories:** 210 kcal
- » **Total Fats:** 8 g
- » **Saturated Fats:** 5 g

- » **Cholesterol:** 25 mg
- » **Sodium:** 140 mg
- » **Carbs:** 27 g
- » **Fibers:** 1 g
- » **Sugar:** 18 g
- » **Proteins:** 5 g

10. Watermelon Lime Sorbet

Prep Time: 20 minutes
Cook Time: 5 minutes
Total Time: 25 minutes
Serving: 1
Level: 1

Ingredients:

- » 1 tbsp water
- » ¾ cup seedless watermelon
- » 1 tbsp food thickener
- » 2 tsp lime juice
- » 2 ½ tsp sugar

Instructions:

1. In a pan, mix the sugar and water. Stirring as the sugar melts under the broiler.
2. Watermelon should be pureed until smooth after all white seeds are removed.
3. Blend thoroughly after adding the sugar/water combination and lime juice.
4. When the mixture begins to thicken and the powder is mixed, put food thickener, then blend until combined.
5. Put into a small pan or basin. Freeze when covered.
6. Sorbet should be taken out of the freezer and let to defrost until it is just barely slushy before serving. A spoon/fork might be used to shave the sorbet till it is sufficiently soft to scoop.

Nutrients:

- » **Calories:** 90 kcal
- » **Total Fats:** 0 g
- » **Saturated Fats:** 0 g
- » **Cholesterol:** 0 mg
- » **Sodium:** 10 mg
- » **Carbs:** 24 g
- » **Fibers:** 0 g
- » **Sugar:** 10 g
- » **Proteins:** 1 g

11. Luck of the Irish Milkshake

Prep Time: 5 minutes
Cook Time: 0 minutes
Total Time: 5 minutes
Serving: 1
Level: 3

Ingredients:

- 4 oz container frozen dessert vanilla
- 1 cup thickened dairy drink, honey vanilla
- whipped cream, for topping
- 4–5 drops green food coloring
- ¼ tsp mint extract

Instructions:

1. Blend all the ingredients until they are completely smooth.
2. Put into 1 glass, and when desired, top it with whipped cream and green decorator sugar.

Nutrients:

- **Calories:** 470 kcal
- **Total Fats:** 16 g
- **Saturated Fats:** 10 g
- **Cholesterol:** 25 mg
- **Sodium:** 350 mg
- **Carbs:** 64 g
- **Fibers:** 0 g
- **Sugar:** 46 g
- **Proteins:** 17 g

12. Lava Cakes

Prep Time: 15 minutes
Cook Time: 35 minutes
Total Time: 50 minutes
Serving: 1
Level: 3

Ingredients:

- ½ tbsp vegetable oil
- 2 tbsp bread and dessert mix texture modified
- 1 tsp cocoa powder
- 2 tsp chocolate syrup
- 1 tsp chocolate syrup used for lava sauce
- 3 tbsp milk
- ¾ tsp sugar

Instructions:

1. Put non-stick spray into muffin cups just enough to coat them.
2. Combine the dessert and texture-modified bread in a bowl. In a mixing basin, combine sugar and cocoa powder.
3. When the mixture looks like wet sand, put oil, then stir.
4. Stir in the first stated amount of the chocolate syrup to boiling milk.
5. The mixture will start to thicken once you quickly whisk in the milk.

6. Using a scoop, put into the cups for muffins, then distribute evenly.
7. For at least 30 minutes, cover and leave the dish at room temperature or in the refrigerator.
8. Place the prepared cake onto a serving plate after carefully removing them from the muffin cups.
9. Make a little hole on top of every cake using a spoon, then add approximately 1 teaspoon of chocolate syrup.
10. Before serving, add chocolate frosting or whipped cream on top.

Nutrients:
» **Calories:** 210 kcal
» **Total Fats:** 8 g
» **Saturated Fats:** 1.5 g
» **Cholesterol:** 5 mg
» **Sodium:** 100 mg
» **Carbs:** 31 g
» **Fibers:** 1 g
» **Sugar:** 18 g
» **Proteins:** 4 g

13. SNICKERDOODLE COOKIES

Prep Time: 15 minutes
Cook Time: 15 minutes
Total Time: 30 minutes
Serving: 1
Level: 4

Ingredients:
» ½ tsp butter, softened
» ¾ tsp powdered sugar
» ½ tsp cinnamon dash
» 2 tbsp bread and dessert mix texture modified
» 3 tbsp water
» 2 tsp cinnamon sugar
» 1 tsp vegetable oil
» 1 drop almond extract
» 1–2 drops vanilla extract

Instructions:
1. Softened butter plus powdered sugar should be well combined with a mixer.
2. Combine cinnamon with bread and dessert mix (texture Modified) into a separate dish. When the liquid begins to thicken, quickly whisk in almond extract and vanilla extract. Add the mixture to the bread mix.
3. Add to the butter/sugar combination, then combine completely with an electric mixer for about 30 seconds.
4. For 10 to 15 minutes, cover and chill.
5. Use a scoop to portion it into balls, or use a scale to determine 2 tablespoons for each cookie.
6. Every cookie ball should be well covered with cinnamon sugar before being flattened with a broad spatula.

Nutrients:
- **Calories:** 90 kcal
- **Total Fats:** 3.5 g
- **Saturated Fats:** 2 g
- **Cholesterol:** 5 mg
- **Sodium:** 105 mg
- **Carbs:** 14 g
- **Fibers:** 0 g
- **Sugar:** 4 g
- **Proteins:** 3 g

14. Pureed Peanut Butter Blossom Cookies

Prep Time: 15 minutes
Cook Time: 20 minutes
Total Time: 35 minutes
Serving: 1
Level: 4

Ingredients:
- ½ tsp butter
- 2 tbsp creamy peanut butter
- 1 tbsp and 2 tsp bread and dessert mix texture modified
- 1 tsp powdered sugar
- 1 tsp fudge topping
- 2 tbsp water
- ¾ tsp vegetable oil
- 1 drop vanilla extract

Instructions:
1. In a container, combine bread and dessert mix (Texture Modified) with vegetable oil. Stir the mixture just until it looks like wet sand.
2. When the bread mix begins to thicken, quickly whisk in the vanilla extract with the hot water.
3. Until the mixture has cooled, put it in the refrigerator or leave it out at room temperature.
4. Butter that has been softened, peanut butter, and powdered sugar should all be well combined.
5. Blend the addition into the cooled bread mix until well blended.
6. Using a scoop, divide into balls.
7. Spread ½ teaspoon of fudge topping on top of each cookie.

Nutrients:
- **Calories:** 160 kcal
- **Total Fats:** 11 g
- **Saturated Fats:** 2.5 g
- **Cholesterol:** 5 mg
- **Sodium:** 115 mg
- **Carbs:** 14 g
- **Fibers:** 1 g
- **Sugar:** 5 g
- **Proteins:** 4 g

15. Pureed Vanilla Cream Cheese Pumpkin Squares

Prep Time: 20 minutes
Cook Time: 25 minutes
Total Time: 45 minutes
Serving: 1
Level: 3

Ingredients:

- ½ tbsp vegetable oil
- 2 tbsp bread and dessert mix texture modified
- 1 tsp maple syrup
- 1 tbsp pumpkin puree
- 3 tbsp whipped topping
- 2 tbsp water
- ⅛ tsp cinnamon or pumpkin pie spice
- 1 tbsp vanilla pudding
- ½ oz cream cheese

Instructions:

1. Spray the pan thoroughly with non-stick spray for cooking.
2. Pumpkin purée and maple syrup are combined. Place aside.
3. Cinnamon or Pumpkin pie spice should be added with pureed bread and dessert mix. When the mixture looks like wet sand, put oil, then stir.
4. The mixture of the bread and liquid should be quickly stirred to combine.
5. Add the combination of pumpkin and maple syrup.
6. Pour right away into the prepared pan and distribute evenly.
7. For at least 15 minutes, cover and let the food chill at room temperature or in the refrigerator.
8. Cream cheese and pudding should be combined and well mixed. Cover the pumpkin mix in the pan evenly.
9. Put whipped cream on top of the pudding layer.
10. Before cutting and serving, place the pan in the refrigerator or freezer and wrap it with wrapping paper for 30 minutes.

Nutrients:

- **Calories:** 250 kcal
- **Total Fats:** 15 g
- **Saturated Fats:** 6 g
- **Cholesterol:** 15 mg
- **Sodium:** 140 mg
- **Carbs:** 26 g
- **Fibers:** 0 g
- **Sugar:** 14 g
- **Proteins:** 4 g

16. BOLOGNESE SAUCE

Prep Time: 20 minutes
Cook Time: 40 minutes
Total Time: 60 minutes
Serving: 2
Level: 1

Ingredients:
- 1 oz onion
- ½ tbsp sunflower oil
- A pinch oregano
- 1 oz carrots
- 1 tbsp tomato puree
- 3 oz minced beef
- ½ garlic clove
- 1 cup beef stock

Instructions:
1. In a pot with hot oil, gently cook the onions and carrots.
2. When tender, put tomato puree and ground beef, and continue to sauté for a couple of minutes.
3. Pour in the stock, then put the garlic and oregano. Simmer for a while.
4. For around 40 minutes, cook.
5. After allowing it to cool somewhat, combine the sauce into a food processor.

Nutrients:
- **Calories:** 156 kcal
- **Total Fats:** 11 g
- **Saturated Fats:** 3.5 g
- **Cholesterol:** 32 mg
- **Sodium:** 101 mg
- **Carbs:** 4.5 g
- **Fibers:** 1.2 g
- **Sugar:** 2.3 g
- **Proteins:** 11 g

17. CREAMY GARLIC CAULIFLOWER PUREE

Prep Time: 15 minutes
Cook Time: 10 minutes
Total Time: 25 minutes
Serving: 1
Level: 1

Ingredients:
- 1 garlic clove
- 2 cups cauliflower, cooked and chopped
- Salt and pepper, to taste
- 1 tbsp feta, ricotta, or cheese cottage
- 2 tbsp nonfat buttermilk
- 2 tsp olive oil

Instructions:
1. Cauliflower should be chopped into 1-inch pieces and boiled for 10 minutes or until fork-mashable.
2. When the mixture is creamy and smooth, add all the components to a blender and blend until combined.
3. If you want, you may also include cottage, feta, or ricotta cheese.
4. If preferred, add chives as a garnish, then serve in a dish.

Nutrients:
- **Calories:** 204 kcal
- **Total Fats:** 17 g
- **Saturated Fats:** 10 g
- **Cholesterol:** 44 mg
- **Sodium:** 696 mg
- **Carbs:** 10 g
- **Fibers:** 5 g
- **Sugar:** 4 g
- **Proteins:** 7 g

18. Pureed Macaroni and Cheese

Prep Time: 20 minutes
Cook Time: 20 minutes
Total Time: 40 minutes
Serving: 4
Level: 1

Ingredients:
- 1 cup milk
- 1 boxed macaroni and cheese kit

Instructions:
1. As usual, prepare the traditional Mac and cheese.
2. Blend a cup of cooked macaroni and cheese.
3. Pour in 1 cup of milk.
4. Till smooth, mix inside a blender.

Nutrients:
- **Calories:** 156 kcal
- **Total Fats:** 10 g
- **Saturated Fats:** 4.4 g
- **Cholesterol:** 23 mg
- **Sodium:** 101 mg
- **Carbs:** 10 g
- **Fibers:** 1.7 g
- **Sugar:** 2.5 g
- **Proteins:** 4 g

19. Pureed Cauliflower

Prep Time: 10 minutes
Cook Time: 5 minutes
Total Time: 15 minutes
Serving: 1
Level: 1

Ingredients:
- Water, as required
- Salt and pepper, to taste
- 1 head chopped cauliflower
- Butter, as your preference

Instructions:
1. The cauliflower should be well-cooked. When it is done, save ½ cup of cooking liquid.
2. Place the cooked cauliflower and cooking water into a blender.
3. To taste, add pepper and salt.
4. Depending on your preference, add a tiny bit of butter.
5. Till smooth, blend.

Nutrients:

- **Calories:** 57 kcal
- **Total Fats:** 0 g
- **Saturated Fats:** 0 g
- **Cholesterol:** 0 mg
- **Sodium:** 0 g
- **Carbs:** 11 g
- **Fibers:** 4 g
- **Sugar:** 2 g
- **Proteins:** 4 g

20. Maple Sweet Potato

Prep Time: 15 minutes
Cook Time: 5 minutes
Total Time: 20 minutes
Serving: 1
Level: 2

Ingredients:

- 1 tbsp milk or cream
- 1 sweet potato
- A pinch cinnamon
- 2 tsp butter
- 2 tsp maple syrup

Instructions:

1. Till the sweet potato is tender, microwave or boil it.
2. Put the potato into a food processor or blender.
3. Add butter, cinnamon, syrup, and cream or milk.
4. Mix thoroughly.

Nutrients:

- **Calories:** 120 kcal
- **Total Fats:** 2.5 g
- **Saturated Fats:** 1.5 g
- **Cholesterol:** 5 mg
- **Sodium:** 190 mg
- **Carbs:** 23 g
- **Fibers:** 3 g
- **Sugar:** 11 g
- **Proteins:** 2 g

21. Cream of Broccoli Soup

Prep Time: 20 minutes
Cook Time: 15 minutes
Total Time: 35 minutes
Serving: 2
Level: 2

Ingredients:

- 2 tbsp oil
- 2 tbsp butter
- 1 cup milk
- Potato flakes, as much as needed for thickening
- 2–3 tbsp flour
- ¼ cup shredded cheese
- 1 frozen broccoli bag

Instructions:

1. Butter, oil, and flour, according to desired thickness, may be combined to make a thick soup foundation.
2. Stirring regularly, heat the mixture slowly until it starts to boil.

3. Mix in a cup full of skim milk gradually.
4. Simmer the new mixture till it thickens.
5. Microwave broccoli till warm and tender while you wait. If necessary, chop in smaller pieces.
6. Blend this foundation with 1 cup of broccoli that has been cooked and a choice of 1/4 cup of cheese that has been shredded. It works well with an electric blender.
7. If desired, put potato flakes for thickening.

Nutrients:
- **Calories:** 147 kcal
- **Total Fats:** 7 g
- **Saturated Fats:** 3 g
- **Cholesterol:** 14 mg
- **Sodium:** 769 mg
- **Carbs:** 17 g
- **Fibers:** 1 g
- **Sugar:** 3 g
- **Proteins:** 6 g

22. BANANA PROTEIN SHAKE

Prep Time: 5 minutes
Cook Time: 0 minutes
Total Time: 5 minutes
Serving: 1
Level: 1

Ingredients:
- 1 cup Greek yogurt
- 1 cup almond milk
- Ice, as required
- 1 banana frozen
- 1 scoop vanilla protein powder
- ⅛ tsp ground cinnamon

Instructions:
1. Blend the almond milk, banana, Greek yogurt, ice, vanilla powder, and cinnamon.
2. Until smooth, blend.
3. Add extra almond milk into your blender when the smoothie seems too thick.

Nutrients:
- **Calories:** 171 kcal
- **Total Fats:** 8.5 g
- **Saturated Fats:** 1.3 g
- **Cholesterol:** 12 mg
- **Sodium:** 212 mg
- **Carbs:** 2.5 g
- **Fibers:** 1.2 g
- **Sugar:** 1.8 g
- **Proteins:** 19 g

23. Strawberry Protein Shake

Prep Time: 5 minutes
Cook Time: 0 minutes
Total Time: 5 minutes
Serving: 1
Level: 1

Ingredients:

- ¼ cup Greek yogurt
- ½ cup almond milk
- ½ scoop vanilla whey protein powder
- Honey or stevia, to taste
- 3 strawberries
- 3 ice cubes

Nutrients:

- **Calories:** 415 kcal
- **Total Fats:** 3 g
- **Saturated Fats:** 2 g
- **Cholesterol:** 13 mg
- **Sodium:** 197 mg
- **Carbs:** 69 g
- **Fibers:** 1.8 g
- **Sugar:** 66 g
- **Proteins:** 24 g

Instructions:

1. Blend all of the components.
2. Until smooth, blend.
3. If the mixture gets too thick, put almond milk.

Chapter 6

30-Day Meal Plan

In this chapter, there is a 30-days meal plan for you to follow and have a healthy diet if you have dysphagia. It includes all the recipes that you can eat for your breakfast, lunch, snack, and dinner.

Day 1:
- Breakfast: Pureed Sausage Gravy and Biscuits
- Lunch: Fresh Pea Soup
- Snack: Savory Beet Puree
- Dinner: Easy-Peasy Chicken

Day 2:
- Breakfast: Pureed Berry Muffins
- Lunch: Lima Bean Purée
- Snack: Sweet Apple Bread Puree
- Dinner: Lobster Bisque

Day 3:
- Breakfast: Thickened Brown Sugar Milk Tea
- Lunch: Pumpkin Cauliflower Curry
- Snack: Decadent dessert
- Dinner: Beef and Sweet Potato Puree with Thyme

Day 4:
- Breakfast: Apple, squash and Turkey Sausage Hash (Moist and Minced)
- Lunch: Chili
- Snack: Watermelon Sorbet
- Dinner: Minced Meat Shepherd's Pie

Day 5:
- Breakfast: Basted Eggs
- Lunch: Chicken a la King
- Snack: Minted Melon Smoothie
- Dinner: Sweet and Sour Chicken

Day 6:
- Breakfast: Coconut Mango Puree
- Lunch: Turkey Tetrazzini
- Snack: Vanilla Cake
- Dinner: Soft Potatoes

Day 7:
- Breakfast: Bread Stuffing
- Lunch: Pureed Pasta with Beef Marinara
- Snack: Chocolate Cake
- Dinner: Pureed Pasta with Chicken Alfredo

Day 8:
- » Breakfast: Cranberry Almond Bread
- » Lunch: Vegetable Fried Rice
- » Snack: Vanilla Cake
- » Dinner: Country BBQ Sundae

Day 9:
- » Breakfast: Cranberry Pear Tart
- » Lunch: Hamburger and Bun
- » Snack: Thickened Mocha Latte
- » Dinner: BBQ Pork

Day 10:
- » Breakfast: Pureed Broccoli, Cheese, and Egg Dish
- » Lunch: Pureed Cornbread
- » Snack: Thickened Pumpkin Spice Latte
- » Dinner: Spiced carrot and lentil soup

Day 11:
- » Breakfast: Chocolate Avocado Pudding
- » Lunch: Beef Stroganoff
- » Snack: Watermelon Lime Sorbet
- » Dinner: Cullen skink

Day 12:
- » Breakfast: Apple Crumble
- » Lunch: Minced Turkey Tetrazzini
- » Snack: Luck of the Irish Milkshake
- » Dinner: Pureed Green Bean Casserole

Day 13:
- » Breakfast: Baked Custard
- » Lunch: Pureed Pasta with Beef Marinara
- » Snack: Lava Cakes
- » Dinner: Pureed Lasagna

Day 14:
- » Breakfast: Maple Sweet Carrot Puree
- » Lunch: Corned Beef and Cabbage
- » Snack: Snickerdoodle Cookies
- » Dinner: Squash, Apple and Turkey Sausage Hash

Day 15:
- » Breakfast: Pumpkin Brownie Puree
- » Lunch: White Sauce Pasta Recipe
- » Snack: Pureed Peanut Butter Blossom Cookies
- » Dinner: Pureed Cheesy Vegetable Dish

Day 16:
- » Breakfast: Peach Apricot Puree
- » Lunch: Pureed Lemon Cream Cheese Pie
- » Snack: Pureed Vanilla Cream Cheese Pumpkin Squares
- » Dinner: Creamy Fortified Butternut Squash Soup

Day 17:
- » Breakfast: Fig Berry Puree
- » Lunch: Meat Loaf Puree
- » Snack: Bolognese Sauce
- » Dinner: Turkey and Dumpling Soup

Day 18:
- » Breakfast: Peaches and Cream
- » Lunch: Chicken Tikka Masala with Sticky Rice
- » Snack: Creamy Garlic Cauliflower Puree
- » Dinner: Chicken Croquettes with Mashed Potatoes

Day 19:
- » Breakfast: Frozen Yogurt Parfait
- » Lunch: Roasted Cauliflower Macaroni and Cheese
- » Snack: Pureed Macaroni and Cheese
- » Dinner: Macaroni and Cheese

Day 20:
- » Breakfast: Scrambled Egg and Bean Puree
- » Lunch: Black Bean Soup
- » Snack: Pureed Cauliflower
- » Dinner: Cold-Day Chicken Noodle Soup

Day 21:
- » Breakfast: Pureed Egg Salad
- » Lunch: Italian Chicken Puree
- » Snack: Maple Sweet Potato
- » Dinner: Potatoes with Cheddar

Day 22:
- » Breakfast: Scrambled Eggs
- » Lunch: Black Bean and Red Pepper Puree
- » Snack: Cream of Broccoli Soup
- » Dinner: Grilled Cheese and Pickle Sandwich

Day 23:
- » Breakfast: Scrambled Eggs
- » Lunch: Pureed Salmon
- » Snack: Banana Protein Shake
- » Dinner: Braised Carrots

Day 24:
- » Breakfast: Frozen Yogurt Parfait
- » Lunch: Pureed Salmon
- » Snack: Strawberry Protein Shake
- » Dinner: Lyonnaise Potatoes

Day 25:
- » Breakfast: Pureed Berry Muffins
- » Lunch: Pumpkin Cauliflower Curry
- » Snack: Cream of Broccoli Soup
- » Dinner: Turkey Burgers with Roasted Sweet Potatoes

Day 26:
- » Breakfast: Thickened Brown Sugar Milk Tea
- » Lunch: Chili
- » Snack: Strawberry Protein Shake
- » Dinner: Pumpkin Crisp

Day 27:
- » Breakfast: Basted Eggs
- » Lunch: Chicken a la King
- » Snack: Banana Protein Shake
- » Dinner: Tangy Chicken Salad

Day 28:
- » Breakfast: Coconut Mango Puree
- » Lunch: Turkey Tetrazzini
- » Snack: Snickerdoodle Cookies
- » Dinner: Basic Fish Puree

Day 29:
- » Breakfast: Bread Stuffing
- » Lunch: Pureed Pasta with Beef Marinara
- » Snack: Banana Protein Shake
- » Dinner: Pureed Beef Stew

Day 30:
- » Breakfast: Cranberry Almond Bread
- » Lunch: Hamburger and Bun
- » Snack: Snickerdoodle Cookies
- » Dinner: Tuna and Beans Puree

Where to Find Special Products for the above Recipes?

Following are some websites or stores where you can buy these products such as thickeners, thickened tea, texture-modified, etc.

- » Vitality Medical
- » Walmart
- » Amazon
- » Vital Medical Supplies
- » Thick it
- » Walgreens
- » Martin's Super Markets

Conclusion

Numerous muscles and neurons collaborate to move food or liquid from our lips into our bellies during swallowing. Swallowing issues can come from any place in the mouth, pharynx, or esophagus. A muscle tunnel in your pharynx called the esophagus transports food and liquids from your mouth to the stomach. Swallowing issues can range from minor to serious. The method of therapy differs according to the problem's root cause. To assist you in breathing, physicians will occasionally recommend medicine. After being identified with dysphagia, people may be advised to follow a "texture-modified diet," or specifically adapted cuisine. Food and beverages with modified viscosity and soft texture are typically safer and simpler for those with dysphagia to ingest.

A caregiver can assist by choosing where to have dinner, what to consume while out, or by including someone they love in meal preparation. In addition to boosting self-esteem, it encourages salivation, which will aid in ingesting when necessary. Patience and taking time while dining with someone you love are important strategies. An open call for choking or aspiration is eating quickly. Motivate the person to consume smaller portions more frequently and, if at all feasible, in smaller quantities. Sometimes frailty and exhaustion make it difficult to breathe, which upsets a person you love. If they have dysphagia, their balance while consuming and imbibing is very essential. Getting both feet level on the floor and sitting erect will aid in inhaling and eating. To lessen the likelihood of stomach problems developing, a caregiver must assist a loved one in remaining erect for 30–45 minutes after meals. While social interaction during meals is important, it can be risky for the person you love who has dysphagia. Talking and breathing are intertwined, so when someone is eager to share something, it's simple for them to neglect food or beverage. They also need to be swallowing. Most people dislike being told, discussed, or forced to adjust their daily schedules or diets. It frequently entails an impairment of some kind, whether it be the pleasure of meals they have grown accustomed to over time or general independence, particularly during festivals and family gatherings. While the loved ones may complain that they're once again consuming baby food, a caregiver can help eliminate these unfavorable perceptions by stressing how crucial these modifications are to their very survival. Life requires adequate nourishment and water, and depending on how severe the eating issue is, the alterations may not be long-lasting. Someone you love with dysphagia may enjoy a satisfying social life and avoid further problems down the road through a changed diet, counseling, or even just greater consciousness.

Conversion Table

Kitchen Conversion Guide

Dry Measurement

CUPS	TABLESPOON	TEASPOON	GRAMS / POUNDS
4	64	192	2 pounds
2	32	96	1 pound
1	16	48	128
3/4	12	36	96
2/3	10 2/3	32	85

Liquid Measurement

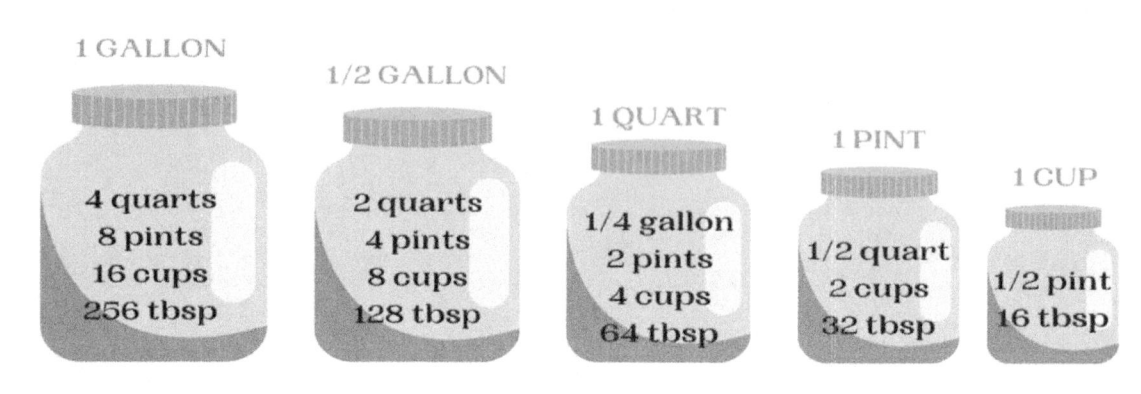

1 GALLON
4 quarts
8 pints
16 cups
256 tbsp

1/2 GALLON
2 quarts
4 pints
8 cups
128 tbsp

1 QUART
1/4 gallon
2 pints
4 cups
64 tbsp

1 PINT
1/2 quart
2 cups
32 tbsp

1 CUP
1/2 pint
16 tbsp

Oven Measurement

°F	500	475	450	425	400	375
°C	260	240	230	220	200	190

Made in United States
North Haven, CT
02 August 2023